GRACE:
The DNA *of* GOD

What the Bible Says About Grace
and Its Life-Transforming Power

TONY COOKE

Harrison House

14 13 12 11   10 9 8 7 6 5 4 3 2 1

Grace: The DNA of God
What the Bible Says About Grace and Its Life-Transforming Power
ISBN 978-1-60683-314-8

Copyright © 2011 by Tony Cooke
Tony Cooke is represented by Thomas J. Winters of Winters & King, Inc., Tulsa, Oklahoma.
Published by Harrison House, Inc.
P. O. Box 35035
Tulsa, Oklahoma 74153

WHAT PEOPLE ARE SAYING...

Grace is one of the most misunderstood concepts in the Church today, and yet it is one of the most important. From personal study, the wisdom of church leaders, and the revelation of God's Word, Tony Cooke illuminates grace as God's empowerment to live in His glory. This book is a powerful resource in recognizing and receiving all that God has given us.

-**John Bevere**, Author/Speaker
Messenger International
Colorado Springs/Australia/United Kingdom

Shamefully, my initial reaction before reading Tony's manuscript was "Oh, another book about grace. Haven't we had enough of those?" Dutifully, I picked it up and began to read. I soon was repenting of my cynical thoughts as Tony's insights, garnered over 25 years of engagement with this vital topic, poured off the pages into my heart. *What a treasure*, I thought, *and how readable and engaging and exhaustive*. Tony turns over grace like a polished gem, examining five gorgeous facets that empower and enable our walk with God. What you end up with is not a cheap "get out of jail free card," but rather a profound, balanced understanding of grace and its role in perfecting obedience, holiness, and responsibility in our lives. This is a rich and powerful read that you will find lively, illuminating, and enriching to your personal world.

-**Dr. Berin Gilfillan**
Founder and President of the International School of Ministry

I am confident that *Grace: The DNA of God* will become a classic on the subject of grace. In this day and age, when the subject of grace is being strangely twisted and distorted beyond my ability to comprehend, Tony's book is "on time" to confront confusion on this subject that is being propagated in various quarters of the

Body of Christ. I find this book so helpful, that I wish to say, "Tony, thank you for this great job and for your bravery to raise your written voice on this seriously misunderstood but life-changing subject." For anyone looking for solid answers about the grace of God, this is the place to start. Pastors and leaders look no further, for in this book you will find balanced biblical, doctrinally correct answers to help you confront the maze of heresy that seems to be finding its way into the mainstream of the Church. And if you are not in a leadership role but are hungry to know the truth about grace, you can confidently open your eyes, ears, and mind to what is contained in *Grace: The DNA of God*. As a pastor, teacher, television host, head of a large association of churches, and president of a seminary, I assure you that this book will become required reading by those we lead and mentor. I have read it cover to cover, and I recommend it with great enthusiasm.

-Rick Renner
Author and Pastor of Good News Church, Moscow, Russia

If one were to inquire what the most celebrated yet misunderstood subject Christendom currently faces, with little argument it would be the holy and ill-handled subject of the grace of God. In *Grace: The DNA of God* Tony Cooke has not only masterfully explained but proven by biblical precedent that grace does not mean that Heaven is void of opinion, nor is all overlooked because of the crimson flow. Grace is the road of humility men travel that reveals their authenticity, but also it is the power given to them to become a mature "son" in God's celestial family. Enjoy with godly reverence these pages with me as we soak in accuracy and drink together of God's amazing grace.

-Dr. Robb Thompson
Pastor of Family Harvest Church in Tinley Park, Illinois

Any Christian who has walked with the Lord over a period of time realizes with humility and gratefulness that his or her life is centered on the grace of God. Tony Cooke has given us one of the greatest explanations of grace in his book *Grace: The DNA of God*. This book gives sound teaching that corrects the misunderstanding that some have had regarding grace. I recommend this book to every believer who desires to know truth.

-Sharon Daugherty
Senior Pastor of Victory Christian Center, Tulsa, Oklahoma

In his new book, *Grace: The DNA of God*, my friend Rev. Tony Cooke has thoroughly and simply presented the biblical teaching concerning the grace of God. Tony examines grace from the Old Testament through the teaching of the New Testament writers, showing that grace is not a new subject but the very "DNA of God." The apostle Peter wrote, as recorded in 1 Peter 4:10, that grace is many-sided, and Tony has examined the sides of grace in a systematic yet interesting manner that will enthusiastically move the reader from chapter to chapter with great anticipation. I am confident Tony has written a book that will help the body of Christ better understand the important subject of grace, and in doing so, better understand the Author of that grace, God the Father. Rev. Tony Cooke was my associate at Rhema Bible Church for nineteen years, and it is a pleasure for me to recommend his new book, *Grace: The DNA of God*.

-Rev. Kenneth W. Hagin
President of Kenneth Hagin Ministries
Pastor of Rhema Bible Church, Broken Arrow, Oklahoma

Tony Cooke has hit a grand slam in *Grace: The DNA of God*. At last the body of Christ can have an honest and understandable revelation of God's transforming power through grace. He gently teaches us what grace is not, then proceeds to coach us in the realities and possibilities of experiencing God's genuine grace. Tony has a gift for taking misunderstood topics and, without condemnation, bringing the truth to the hearts of people in a simple, understandable manner.

-Pastor Dave Williams
Mount Hope Church, Lansing, Michigan

The subject of grace is the very foundation of the New Covenant. Grace is also so multi-faceted that it is imperative to rightly divide this subject. In *Grace: The DNA of God*, Tony has done a masterful job of exploring and explaining the entire spectrum of God's grace. Often in dealing with such a vital Bible subject, the end result is complicated or excessive; however, Tony has successfully presented the Gospel of the grace of God in a manner that will be clear and easy to understand for anyone and everyone. Truth, by definition, will always make one free. This book will surely free any reader from excess of either legalism or liberalism into the real purpose of the grace of God.

-Pastor Mark Brazee
World Outreach Church, Tulsa, Oklahoma

The principle of grace is a part of the core curriculum of Scripture; it is a truth that every believer must grasp. The shear volume of verses in the Old and New Testaments elevate the subject of grace into the "need-to-know" category. Personally, I cannot think of anyone better to cover the doctrine of grace than Tony Cooke. First, his adherence to sound standards of biblical interpretation is a breath of fresh air, especially in a day when extremes have become the norm. Second, his hands-on experience in pastoral ministry provides valuable perspectives in the practical application of grace. As a pastor, I think Tony's breakdown on the five kinds of grace is masterful. This book should be required reading for every Bible student. It provides clear insight into one of the greatest biblical concepts.

-Pastor Gerald Brooks, D.D.

Grace Outreach Center, Plano, Texas

Tony Cooke has masterfully produced this much-needed work. Major Bible truths often get lost to the "sound bite" world of modern presentation. This book is not only exhaustive in its coverage, but could easily stand as a textbook in any Bible school. Simple yet complete, my hat goes off to Tony for this timely work. The Church needs more study. The Church needs in-depth perspective. Thank you, Tony, for this contribution.

-Pastor Randy Gilbert

Faith Landmarks Ministries, Richmond, Virginia

Grace is an unavoidable issue throughout the Bible. We are who we are, accomplish what we do, and reach our full potential by His grace. Grace is multifaceted in its colors, sorts, and expressions. In his book *Grace: The DNA of God* Tony Cooke carries us on a skillfully crafted and practical journey into the manifold grace of God. This book is a must read for the called, all who are pursuers, and those standing in the grace of God.

-Dr. LaFayette Scales

Rhema Christian Center, Columbus, Ohio

Tony Cooke's book is a Godsend in this hour. The Bible warns us of people who try to turn God's grace into something it is not (Jude 4) to free themselves of being the godly people we should be. Read this book if you want to live responsible, resourced and rewarded by God! And give it to anyone you want to equip to live in God's best.

-Pastor Jim Graff
Faith Family Church
President, Significant Church Network

God's grace is truly transformational. Tony Cooke does a marvelous job of thoroughly addressing the various questions and confusion on the topic of God's grace. I especially like that he does not back away from some hard scriptures, digging into the Word in the Spirit of truth. As a professional working with believers who are troubled in one aspect of life or another, I wish all could truly grasp the truth about grace that is discussed in these pages, for if they would, it would radically transform them, their relationships, and their world.

-Stuart Holderness, Ph.D.
Stuart Holderness & Associates, Tulsa, Oklahoma

Dedication

To my wife, Lisa. I'm so thankful that the Lord made us heirs together of the grace of life. You have brought joy to our journey and to my heart in countless ways.

CONTENTS

How Do I Grow in God's Grace?

What's the Controversy About Grace?

One More Thing You Should Know...

A NOTE FROM THE AUTHOR

I was eighteen and had just had a wonderful encounter with God. My mother's friend Marjorie, who had been in church her entire life, was excited to hear about it. Then she dropped the bomb. "I wonder if you could help me understand something. I have never been able to grasp the meaning of the word *grace*."

Two things came to my mind. First was the hymn everyone knows: "Amazing Grace." Second was the definition everyone hears: unmerited favor. Knowing very little, but hoping to appear halfway intelligent, I decided to go with the latter. "Grace is unmerited favor," I told her.

"What does that mean?"

I realized I had tried to define something she did not understand by using another phrase she did not understand. I said, "Unmerited favor is favor we haven't merited." Things were not getting any clearer—to her or to me! But I was hooked. I had to find a satisfactory answer. At the time, I didn't realize how long it would take.

As I continued reading the Bible over the years, I took note of references to grace and began to gain small bits of insight. The truth about grace began to reveal certain insecurities and "misbeliefs" in my life. Even though I realized it was by God's grace I had become His child, I had somehow come to think that my continued acceptance with God was based on me doing everything perfectly. I also realized that I had been trying to live the Christian life in my own strength. I knew God loved me enough to save me, but as I struggled with my flesh and the world, sometimes failing, I saw Him as angry, judgmental, and disappointed in me. Through this misperception, I saw Him not as my loving Father and Helper but as a mere faultfinder.

I knew God's grace was lovingly supplied for my initiation into His kingdom, but I had no idea God also lovingly supplied grace for my continuation in His kingdom. Eventually, as I studied grace more in-depth, I began to see the truth: After being saved it was still His grace that made me His, kept me His, and would enable me to live in a way that pleased Him. The growing reservoir of grace in me produced more and more strength, wisdom, and joy. I found old areas of fear, guilt, shame, and condemnation dropping away. I had begun to discover the joy of grace-based living.

In 1986, I preached about grace for the first time. Shortly after that I shared a few sessions on the topic of grace at a ministers' conference. Then I taught a course entitled "Understanding Grace" at a Bible school from 1988-1994. The grace of God has been percolating in my heart for a long time, and I am still excited as I continue to learn and grow in it!

In recent years, I have been delighted to hear more and more ministers teaching on the grace of God not just for initiation into the kingdom but continuation in the kingdom. At the same time, I have been disturbed to observe some misapplying God's grace by discounting other New Testament truths that are essential to living a life that is pleasing to God.

I'm not out to attack any ministers or get on a soapbox about "all the error being taught." My heart's desire is simply to present the revelation of grace as the Holy Spirit has revealed it in His Word. Then you can study and decide for yourself what is biblical teaching and what is not.

As you read, remember that God is completely committed to you. Don't just read for information but seek the transformation He offers.

My prayer is that you will truly "taste and see that the LORD is good" (Psalm 34:8). I believe that insecurities and fears you have battled will be eradicated as you understand and embrace God's grace in your life. His grace will empower you with His divine confidence and compassion, and you will be radically changed.

Tony Cooke
April 2011

Part One

WHY STUDY GRACE?

Chapter 1

GOD'S DNA IN YOU

A Christian has God's DNA.

Those were the words on a church sign—the kind where they change the message each week. That's hardly a message etched on granite tablets by the finger of God, but it is thought-provoking. After all, the apostle John said, "Beloved, now we are children of God" (1 John 3:2). If we inherit our genes physically from our parents, then maybe we inherit something of God's spiritual nature when we are born of Him.

Physically speaking, DNA is a molecule that resides in each of the hundred trillion cells in your body and each strand of DNA contains the blueprint—the genetic instructions—that enable your body to live, develop, and function. A renowned medical doctor wrote: "DNA is estimated to contain instructions that, if written out, would fill a thousand six-hundred-page books."[1] You truly are "fearfully and wonderfully made" (Psalm 139:14).

Maybe it's been a long time since you studied that funny twisted-ladder looking type of thing in Biology class called a double helix, but you've probably heard about DNA more recently in connection to evidence used in criminal investigations on television. Because each of us has completely unique DNA (unless you're an identical twin), DNA has become useful in resolving paternity issues and in helping to establish guilt or innocence in certain crimes.

When each of us was conceived, we received our genetic makeup from our parents. As we grew and developed physically, the traits and characteristics that had been encoded in our DNA became apparent. A fertilized egg became an embryo, a fetus, an infant, a toddler, and eventually, an adult.

In scientific terms, the genetic code we received from our parents is called our "genotype." The genotype refers to the internal code or blueprint within our cells that produces an outward manifestation or expression called our "phenotype." In other words, our phenotype is what can be observed externally, such as our hair color, height, body frame, etc., all of which were defined in our DNA.

This becomes especially fascinating when we consider the parallel between the natural and the spiritual. Jesus not only said, "God is Spirit" (John 4:24), but also said (speaking in context of the new birth), "That which is born of the flesh is flesh, and that which is born of the Spirit is spirit" (John 3:6). Physically, we received our DNA through our parents, but spiritually, our human spirit has been born of God and regenerated by His Spirit. As we grow and develop spiritually, we will express more and more of His nature and character that we received in our new birth.

Can We Really Share in God's Nature?

According to Genesis 1:26, the first words that came from the mouth of God about man were, "Let Us make man in Our image, according to Our likeness." One commentary states, "Being in God's image means that humans share, though imperfectly and finitely, in God's nature, that is, in His communicable attributes (life, personality, truth, wisdom, love, holiness, justice), and so have the capacity for spiritual fellowship with Him."[2]

Us sharing God's nature? That is a bold statement, but Scripture reinforces this idea consistently.

- Paul says believers, "...have put on the new self, which is being re-newed in knowledge in the image of its Creator" (Colossians 3:10, NIV). Paul also admonished the Ephesians to, "...put on the new nature (the regenerate self) created in God's image, [Godlike] in true righteousness and holiness" (Ephesians 4:24, AMP).

- Peter tells us that it is through God's "exceedingly great and pre-cious promises" that we become "partakers of the divine nature" (2 Peter 1:4).

- Seven times in his first epistle, John refers to believers as those who are "born of God."

- John and Paul make several references to us being "the children of God" and Paul states, "you are all sons of God through faith in Christ Jesus" (Galatians 3:26).

- Paul also made a most startling statement when he said, "...if any-one is in Christ, he is a new creation; old things have passed away; behold, all things have become new" (2 Corinthians 5:17).

It is one thing to receive the nature of God through the new birth (genotype)—like the sign said, "A Christian Has God's DNA." But it is another thing altogether to give vibrant expression of His nature through our lives as we grow and develop spiritually (phenotype). We've all known Christians who have been spiritually barren—not expressing much of God's nature outwardly. But God wants us to "reflect the glory of the Lord" and become "more and more like him as we are changed into his glorious image" (2 Corinthians 3:18 NLT).

God's grace is integrally involved in both of these processes. It is through the grace of God that we are born again, and it is through the grace of God that we are enabled to express His nature (His love, mercy, compassion, etc.) through our lives toward others.

When we refer to grace as God's DNA, we are simply saying that God is gracious, and that His grace—His nature—was conveyed to us spiritually when we became His children. In the journey ahead, we are going to explore not only how God's love and grace are imparted into our lives, but also what His grace produces in and through us, and how His nature and character are expressed through our lives.

Chapter 2

GRACE IN
SCRIPTURE

*And as God's grace reaches more and more people, there will be great
thanksgiving, and God will receive more and more glory.*

2 Corinthians 4:15 NLT

Generally speaking, the value and importance of a doctrine can
be measured by how much emphasis the Bible places on it. If
the Bible says a lot about it, then we should probably say a lot
about it as well. As I surveyed the usage of the term *grace* in the Bible,
I was impressed with two facts. First, grace is seen operating continuously throughout Scripture. Second, grace has enormous scope. It is deep,
broad, and powerful. The extent of its actions and how much it produces
is nearly incomprehensible.

Because of its frequent use in Scripture, grace should be an oft-
preached topic, and a frequent subject of discussion among believers.
Consider the following descriptions of grace found in the Bible. Like me,
I believe you will be amazed to see the awesome nature of God's grace
and what it actually does in you, for you, and through you.

- The Lord is gracious (Psalm 111:4).

- He is the giver of grace (Proverbs 3:34).

- He is the God of all grace (1 Peter 5:10).

- His throne is a throne of grace (Hebrews 4:16).

- The Holy Spirit is called the Spirit of grace (Hebrews 10:29).

- Our message is called "The Gospel of the Grace of God" and "The Word of His Grace" (Acts 20:24, 32).

- The prophets of old prophesied of the grace that should come to us (1 Peter 1:10). This grace came by Jesus (John 1:17).

- Jesus was full of grace, and it is from His fullness that we receive one grace after another (John 1:14,16).

- The grace of God was upon Jesus and gracious words proceeded out of His mouth (Luke 2:40; 4:22).

- It was by grace that Jesus tasted of death for every man (Hebrews 2:9).

We are told to:

- Continue in grace (Acts 13:43).

- Abound in grace (2 Corinthians 8:7).

- Be strong in grace (2 Timothy 2:1).

- Grow in grace (2 Peter 3:18).

The Word of God speaks of:

- Great grace (Acts 4:33).

- The abundance of grace (Romans 5:17).

- The exceeding grace of God (2 Corinthians 9:14).

- The glory of His grace (Ephesians 1:6).

- The riches of His grace (Ephesians 1:7).

- The exceeding riches of His grace (Ephesians 2:7).

- The dispensation of the grace of God (Ephesians 3:2).

- The gift of the grace of God (Ephesians 3:7).

- The grace of life (1 Peter 3:7).

- The manifold grace of God (1 Peter 4:10).

- The true grace of God (1 Peter 5:12).

Grace can be:

- Found (Genesis 6:8; Hebrews 4:16).

- Shown (Ezra 9:8).

- Poured (Psalm 45:2).

- Received (Romans 1:5).

- Seen and perceived (Acts 11:23; Galatians 2:9).

Grace saves us and empowers us to live a life pleasing to God:

- We are saved by grace and through grace (Acts 15:11; Ephesians 2:8).

- It is through the grace of God that we believe (Acts 18:27).

- Grace builds us up and gives us an inheritance (Acts 20:32).

- We are justified freely by His grace (Romans 3:24).

- Grace makes the promise sure to all those who are of faith (Romans 4:16).

- Paul ministered through the grace that was given to him (Romans 12:3).

- We have gifts differing according to the grace that is given to us (Romans 12:6).

- Grace causes us to be enriched by Him in all utterance and in all knowledge (1 Corinthians 1:4-5).

- Grace makes us what we are and works in us and through us (1 Corinthians 15:10).

- It is the grace of God that makes us rich (2 Corinthians 8:9).

- God's grace is sufficient for us and causes us to reign in life (2 Corinthians 12:9; Romans 5:17).

- We are called by grace into grace (Galatians 1:6,15).

- Grace enables us to preach the unsearchable riches of Christ (Ephesians 3:8).

- Our words can impart grace to others (Ephesians 4:29).

- We are partakers of grace (Philippians 1:7).

- We sing with grace in our hearts, and our words are to be seasoned with grace (Colossians 3:16; 4:6).

- Grace gives us everlasting consolation and good hope (2 Thessalonians 2:16).

- Grace teaches us to live holy lives (Titus 2:11-12).

- Grace helps us in time of need (Hebrews 4:16).

- Grace enables us to serve God acceptably (Hebrews 12:28).

- Grace establishes our hearts (Hebrews 13:9).

- Grace is obtained by coming boldly before His throne (Hebrews 4:16).

- Grace is multiplied unto us through the knowledge of God and of Jesus our Lord (2 Peter 1:2).

An individual can:

- Receive grace in vain (2 Corinthians 6:1).

- Set aside or treat as meaningless the grace of God (Galatians 2:21).

- Fall from grace (Galatians 5:4).

- Insult the Spirit of grace (Hebrews 10:29).

- Fall short of grace (Hebrews 12:15).

- Turn the grace of God into lewdness (Jude 4).

Since grace is such a central and continuous theme throughout Scripture, can we really hope to know and understand God and who we are in Christ Jesus without understanding grace? Grace is not a peripheral issue or an afterthought with God; His grace is the essence of who He is and is the basis for how He acts on our behalf. His grace is also the empowering force behind who we become and all we are enabled to do for Him.

Do you see in God's Word that He intended His grace to be thoroughly pervasive and influential in our lives? Every aspect of who we are is to be touched and transformed by His grace. His grace is to guide us and strengthen us in the good times and in the bad, at work and at home, in church and on the streets. His grace is to influence how we relate to Him, to ourselves, and to others.

If grace is this paramount in the Bible, shouldn't it be paramount in your study so that you can find out what it really is and does?

Chapter 3

GRACE IN HELLO.
GRACE IN GOODBYE.

*Grace to you and peace from God our Father
and the Lord Jesus Christ.*

*Grace be with all those who love our
Lord Jesus Christ in sincerity. Amen.*

Ephesians 1:2; 6:24

These two verses are the hello and goodbye in the book of Ephesians. The standard greeting before Jesus came on the scene was *shalom*, the word for God's peace in the Hebrew language.[1] Paul and other New Testament writers added grace (*charis*) to the greeting, making it a very powerful statement. Seventeen times in the New Testament, some variation of "Grace and peace to you" is used in expressing blessing to God's people. In bringing God's grace to mankind, Jesus also brought the peace every Old Testament believer had sought. The fact that grace is always used first indicates that grace is the root of what God did for us through Jesus, while peace follows as the fruit of His gracious work.

There is a depth of meaning every time the Holy Spirit greets us with some form of, "Grace and peace." Today, few understand this. We greet one another with, "Hello! How are you?" But in most cases we are not expecting a revealing or meaningful answer, nor are we saying something profound in our greeting. Likewise, our goodbyes are usually something like, "See ya later," or a simple, "Bye." No weighty communication there! Perhaps this is the reason most of us give little thought to the beginning and ending of the epistles. We assume the writers were simply expressing a formality, and we believe the true substance of Scripture is between what are called the salutations and benedictions.

However, the Word gives us a different perspective. Paul wrote, "All Scripture is given by inspiration of God, and is profitable" (2 Timothy 3:16), and this includes the salutations and benedictions of the epistles. I am convinced they are not superficial formalities. They were inspired by the Holy Spirit to impart powerful spiritual blessing to all who read them.

Hebrews 4:2 also emphasizes the significance of how we respond to Scripture when it says, "The word which they heard did not profit them, not being mixed with faith in those who heard it." We are to profit from all of God's Word, even the hellos and goodbyes! As you read the following salutations and benedictions, personalize them. Allow God to encourage and strengthen you with His grace.

"Grace to you and peace from God our Father and the Lord Jesus Christ." (This phrase occurs ten times in Romans 1:7, 1 Corinthians 1:3, 2 Corinthians 1:2, Galatians 1:3, Ephesians 1:2, Philippians 1:2, Colossians 1:2, 1 Thessalonians 1:1, 2 Thessalonians 1:2, and Philemon 3.)

"The grace of our Lord Jesus Christ be with you." (Similar variations of this phrase occur nine times in Romans 16:20,24; 1 Corinthians 16:23; Galatians 6:18; Philippians 4:23; 1 Thessalonians 5:28; 2 Thessalonians 3:18; Philemon 25; and Revelation 22:21.)

"Grace be with you" (or you all). (This phrase occurs five times in Colossians 4:18; 1 Timothy 6:21; 2 Timothy 4:22; Titus 3:15; and Hebrews 13:25.)

"Grace, mercy, and peace from God our Father and Jesus Christ our Lord." (Similar variations of this phrase occur four times in 1 Timothy 1:2; 2 Timothy 1:2; Titus 1:4; and 2 John 3.)

"The grace of the Lord Jesus Christ, and the love of God, and the communion of the Holy Spirit be with you all." (This phrase occurs one time in 2 Corinthians 13:14.)

"Grace be with all those who love our Lord Jesus Christ in sincerity." (This phrase occurs one time in Ephesians 6:24.)

"Grace and peace be multiplied to you in the knowledge of God and of Jesus our Lord." (This phrase occurs one time in 2 Peter 1:2.)

"Grace to you and peace from Him who is and who was and who is to come." (This phrase occurs one time in Revelation 1:4.)

*   *   *

Say out-loud, "Father, I thank You that this very day, You and the Lord Jesus are releasing grace, peace, and mercy into my life. Thank You that Your grace, Your love, and the communion of the Holy Spirit are mine today." You will be transformed as you realize God's presence through His words of blessing. These are God's thoughts and intentions toward us. He is for us, not against us. None of these letters begin with "Shame, Guilt, and Condemnation to you" because that is not God's heart toward us, grace is. The more we understand grace, the more these salutations and benedictions will mean to us.

Questions for Reflection and Discussion

- What was new and fresh to you?

- What reinforced understanding you already had?

- What challenged your previous or currently held understanding?

- What does the statement, "A Christian has God's DNA," mean to you? How does that affect your life and your attitude toward yourself and other believers?

- Compare and contrast the influence of your physical DNA with your spiritual DNA.

- The frequency of "grace" in Scripture indicates how important it is. What other topics would you think are some of the most often presented and taught in the New Testament?

- After reading through all the "hellos and goodbyes" in the New Testament epistles, how has your understanding of God's grace toward you changed?

- If people do not understand the meaning and significance of grace, is it possible for them to have an accurate understanding of God— who He is, His thoughts toward us, and His plan for our lives? Why or why not?

Part Two

WHAT IS GRACE?

Chapter 4

THE BENEVOLENT JUDGE

Suppose you are driving to work and you are late. All you can think about is getting there as fast as possible, and you are caught on radar going 56 miles an hour where the speed limit is just 35. You are taken to the courthouse to stand before the judge. You are 100 percent guilty, and the fine for going that much over the speed limit is $250. The judge acknowledges your violation of the law and pronounces the sentence. But then something unexpected happens. He reaches into his pocket and personally pays your $250 fine. You are amazed at his kindness and generosity—and breathe a sigh of relief. You are free to go.

As you leave the building, you suddenly realize the judge has followed you outside and is gazing intently at your car, which is an older model with high mileage. Again he reaches into his pocket, only this time he pulls out the keys to a brand new, beautiful car, which is totally paid for and that he drove off the dealership lot the day before. You are in shock. Where did all this favor come from? It certainly had nothing to do with you! The only thing the judge knows about you is that you broke the law. Why did he pay your fine and then give you a new car?

Everything the judge did was based on his character and nature, not on you or your driving performance. You deserved a penalty, but the judge paid it for you, and on top of that, he gave you a brand new car. Now stop and think about how you would respond if such an event actually occurred in your life. Would you drive away from that courthouse bemoaning what a careless driver you had been and mentally grovel about your unworthiness to receive such a fine gift? I don't think so. While you would certainly realize you had been careless in your driving, you would be totally focused on the great generosity and kindness the judge had extended toward you. You would forever love, honor, respect, and appreciate him. Your new devotion to him and high regard for his character would hopefully inspire you to become merciful, gracious, and generous to others, just like he was to you.

This is how God intends for His grace work in your life.

Unmerited Favor Dissected

It has been said, "Mercy is not getting what you deserve, and grace is getting what you don't deserve." It has also been said, "We owed a debt we could not pay, and Jesus paid a debt He did not owe." These statements speak of "unmerited favor" as the definition of God's grace, which is perhaps the most commonly-used definition of grace. Unfortunately, you can focus so heavily on the "unmerited" part that you are unable to enjoy the "favor" of God. Instead of driving away in the new car that was gifted to you, filled with love and devotion for the Benevolent Judge, you might climb back into your old car and drive away under a cloud of guilt and condemnation.

You can dwell so much on your own unworthiness that you hang your head in shame, thinking yourself to be nothing but the proverbial "worm in the dust." You may even wallow perpetually in self-abasement, literally stuck in the mud. If you are living in the shadow of past sins and failures, it is time to change your perspective! The blood of Jesus Christ has cleansed you from all sin and you have been made a child of God. You have a new nature. You need to stop magnifying your past failures and instead magnify His abundant and superior grace. Why? It is His grace that will enable you to overcome your present struggles and move into the future He has for you.

It is completely true that we did nothing to merit or earn the favor of God. To the contrary, we specifically did not merit or deserve it, because all of us have sinned (Romans 3:23). Just like our example of receiving favor after breaking the speed limit, God gave us His favor in spite of ourselves and on the basis of His character and nature—certainly not on the basis of our performance or perfection.

The way to take full advantage of the grace God wants to pour in and through your life is to focus on Him and His grace instead of yourself and your failings. If you perpetually look at yourself (unmerited), you will magnify your faults and flaws; if you focus on Jesus (favor), you will walk in the light of His favor, operating freely in the benefits of His grace and honoring Him for giving His life for you and to you.

Grace Inspires Worship

> There is no word in the New Testament that baffles the expositor
> more than this word "grace." Gather up the occasions in which it
> is found in the New Testament, and read them in their context;
> then sit down in the presence of them, and wonder, and worship.
> —G. Campbell Morgan[1]

Any attempt to define or describe the grace of God should be undertaken with reverential awe and humility. God's grace is so vast, so amazing, and so immeasurable! Our finite minds may feel overwhelmed because God's grace is more than words can convey or imaginations can conceive.

When you thought of yourself driving away from that courthouse totally free and overwhelmingly blessed, your heart was filled with love and awe for that benevolent judge. And the only fitting response to the riches of God's grace, powerfully revealed to you through the death and resurrection of His Son, is to worship and serve the God of all grace for the rest of your life.

We must avoid any fleshly inclination to become proud or arrogant because we think we have achieved some great level of knowledge about God and His grace. In fact, if our understanding of God's grace does not make us more devoted and humble, then we probably do not understand it as well as we think we do!

Paul admonished believers in 1 Corinthians 8:1-2, "Knowledge puffs up, but love edifies. And if anyone thinks that he knows anything, he knows nothing yet as he ought to know." He had admonished us earlier in 1 Corinthians 4:7 NIV, "What do you have that you did not receive?" Insights concerning God's grace are truths He reveals and imparts to us. Though we should certainly study God's Word, His grace is not something we are going to completely grasp apart from Him. And the moment we conclude we have His grace all figured out in our heads, our heart ceases to be open to learn more of who He is, what He has done, and what He desires to do on our behalf—which is all by His grace.

God Does Not Change

Some seem to believe that God was mean and angry in the Old Testament, but somehow became nice in the New Testament. Others seem to believe that there are two different Gods—a God of wrath in the Old Testament and a God of grace in the New Testament. The truth is that God did not undergo a personality change, and there have never been two different Gods. This is why grace is not simply a New Testament concept. The first mention of grace is in the first book of the Bible: "But Noah found grace in the eyes of the LORD" (Genesis 6:8). Over the years I have read various definitions of the word *chen*, the Hebrew word translated *grace* in this verse. It simply implies showing favor, especially when that favor is undeserved. It conveys the idea of one bending or stooping in kindness to bless someone of lesser rank or status. It also carries the idea of help, assistance, and generosity.[2]

Noah and other Old Testament saints experienced the grace and favor of God, but New Testament believers can experience the grace of God in a greatly expanded and intensified way. How did the Holy Spirit define this amazing attribute of God at work in the lives of born-again believers? He used a very special word.

Charis

Grace in the New Testament is in some respects one of its greatest words. It always means two things—God's favor and His blessing; His attitude and His action.

—W. H. Griffith Thomas[3]

The meaning of words can intensify over time. For example, the word "explosion" took on new significance when the atomic bomb was introduced to the world in 1945. The general idea of an explosion remained the same, but the perception of the potential devastation from a single explosion grew exponentially in the minds and imaginations of people across the globe.

The same is true of the Greek word *charis*, which is translated *grace* in English. Before Jesus preached the Gospel of the Kingdom, charis simply referred to something that is beautiful, charming, or pleasant. It described an act of lovingkindness or generosity. Charis was used to depict a person being favorably regarded, the showing of favor, or the giving of a benefit. It was especially used when the favor shown or the kindness exhibited was spontaneous and undeserved.[4] Aristotle defined charis as "helpfulness towards someone in need, not in return for anything, nor that the helper may get anything, but for the sake of the person who is helped."[5]

The outstanding nature of the word charis made it a wonderful choice for Paul and other New Testament writers when they needed a word to describe God's grace: His loving, kind, and benevolent nature was extravagantly expressed toward mankind through His Son, Jesus. However, when charis was applied to the nature of God and His actions toward human beings, this already rich and beautiful word intensified in its grandeur.

Then as today, a person could be benevolent to another without expecting anything in return; but the Greek and Roman gods were rarely benevolent—especially to those who didn't deserve blessing or kindness. Furthermore, the pagan gods always expected something in return for any favor they might happen to give, and many times they were cruel just for the fun of it! That the God of the Bible would show such grace to all sinners—through the sacrifice of His own Son—was utterly astounding!

In the New Testament, charis took on a more splendid and glorious meaning. The concept of grace soared to new heights as it began to express not simply the finite kindnesses of people but the eternal love, compassion, and mercy of the one, true God toward all mankind. This is probably one reason Paul wrote so much about God's grace to the Romans, Galatians, and other churches with Gentile converts. The God of the Bible was totally different from the gods they had worshipped previously. He was the God who offered grace freely to all!

Through the centuries of the Church, the revelation of God's grace has inspired many outstanding descriptions. These insights capture slightly different perspectives and nuances of this amazing attribute of God, His marvelous grace.

Grace is love that cares and stoops and rescues.

—John Stott[6]

Grace and love are, in their innermost essence, one and the same thing.

—Alexander Whyte[7]

Grace is the free, undeserved goodness and favor of God to mankind.

—Matthew Henry[8]

Grace is a proclamation. It is the triumphant announcement that God in Christ has acted and has come to the aid of all who will trust Him for their eternal salvation.

—Lawrence O. Richards[9]

Grace is the very opposite of merit... Grace is not only undeserved favor, but it is favor, shown to the one who has deserved the very opposite.

—Harry Ironside[10]

Grace means more, far more than we can put into words, because it means nothing less than the infinite character of God Himself. It includes mercy for the undeserving and unmerciful, help for the helpless and hopeless, redemption for the renegade and repulsive, love for the unloving and unlovely, kindness for the unkind and unthankful. And all this in full measure and over-flowing abundance, because of nothing in the object, and because of everything in the Giver, God Himself.

—W. H. Griffith Thomas[11]

Chapter 5

FIVE EXPRESSIONS
OF GRACE

Pleasantly enough doth he ride whom the grace of God carrieth. And what marvel if he feeleth no burden who is carried by the Almighty, and is led onwards by the Guide from on High.

—Thomas A Kempis[1]

When Marjorie asked me about the meaning of grace, the only verse of Scripture I could think of was Ephesians 2:8: "For by grace you have been saved through faith, and that not of yourselves; it is the gift of God." It will take eternity to understand the full depth of that verse, and if salvation was the only thing God's grace ever did for us, we could praise Him forever just for that. But there is more to grace. Far more.

As I grew in my understanding of the Bible, I began to notice additional usages of the word *grace* that addressed issues beyond receiving forgiveness for sin and being born-again. At first I just skimmed over those passages, but I eventually realized the Holy Spirit was pointing to the fact that God's grace is not only involved in our initiation into God's family, but His grace is also there to help us in our continuation with God. The grace which saves us also empowers us to live productive and satisfying lives for Him.

John Newton, the author of "Amazing Grace," communicated both of these applications in his famous hymn: "Amazing grace, how sweet the sound, that saved a wretch like me" (initiation). He goes on to write, "'Tis Grace that brought me safe thus far, and grace will lead me home" (continuation). I'm glad the grace that saved me has also brought me this far, and that His grace will continue to lead me until I am home with Him in Heaven. I'm also thankful God's grace was not simply available to me in the past, to be saved, but is a part of me, His nature is now mine, and His grace within is ever-ready to help me live the life He wants me to live.

I want to share five areas where God desires His grace to be at work in our lives. They are not the only areas, but I believe they represent very significant areas in which God desires to transform us, enabling and empowering us to do His will. Each of these pertains to what God does as we yield to and cooperate with Him in these respective areas.

1. **Saving Grace** is God's power and ability to justify us, forgive our sins, and make us new creatures in Jesus Christ.

   For by grace you have been saved through faith, and that not of yourselves; it is the gift of God, not of works, lest anyone should boast.

   Ephesians 2:8-9

2. **Sanctifying Grace** is God's power and ability to purify us and enable us to live holy lives in a corrupt world.

   For the grace of God that brings salvation has appeared to all men, teaching us that, denying ungodliness and worldly lusts, we should live soberly, righteously, and godly in the present age.

   Titus 2:11-12

3. **Strengthening Grace** is God's power and ability to energize and inspire us to live victoriously, to reign over the challenges and circumstances of life.

For if by the one man's offense death reigned through the one, much more those who receive abundance of grace and of the gift of righteousness will reign in life through the One, Jesus Christ.

Romans 5:17

4. Sharing Grace is God's power and ability to meet our needs and take joy in giving to others.

And God is able to make all grace abound toward you, that you, always having all sufficiency in all things, may have an abundance for every good work.

2 Corinthians 9:8

5. Serving Grace is God's power and ability to serve Him and others with His divinely imparted gifts and aptitudes.

As each one has received a gift, minister it to one another, as good stewards of the manifold grace of God.

1 Peter 4:10

- Saving grace keeps us from being lost.

- Sanctifying grace keeps us from being contaminated.

- Strengthening grace keeps us from being defeated.

- Sharing grace keeps us from lack and selfishness.

- Serving grace keeps us from being unproductive.

- Saving grace is the impartation of God's forgiveness.

- Sanctifying grace is the impartation of God's holiness.

- Strengthening grace is the impartation of God's might.

- Sharing grace is the impartation of God's generosity.

- Serving grace is the impartation of God's ability.

The simplest definition I can give of God's grace is this: Grace is love acting. There is nothing passive about God's grace, just like there is nothing passive about His love toward us. God, who is love, has been and continues to act on our behalf, and His love in action is what grace is all about.

In Jeremiah 31:3 NLT, God said to His people, "I have loved you, my people, with an everlasting love. With unfailing love I have drawn you to myself." Can we comprehend what "an everlasting love" is?

- God's love for us has no beginning and no ending.

- God will never stop loving us.

- There is nothing we can do to make God love us more, and there is nothing that we can do to make God love us less.

- He loves us with an everlasting love!

- He draws us to Himself with unfailing love.

If God's grace, in its general sense, is love acting, then:

- Saving grace is Love Rescuing.

- Sanctifying grace is Love Cleansing.

- Strengthening grace is Love Empowering.

- Sharing grace is Love Supplying.

- Serving grace is Love Assisting.

When you understand God's grace as His love acting for you, in you, and through you, you can easily see how grace is more than an intellectual doctrine or theory. His grace is abounding toward you right now; accept and receive it by faith.

One Grace After Another

The apostle John offered this insight into the magnitude of God's grace that was released toward you through Jesus Christ. He said,

> *For out of His fullness (abundance) we have all received [all had a share and we were all supplied with] one grace after another and spiritual blessing upon spiritual blessing and even favor upon favor and gift [heaped] upon gift.*
>
> John 1:16 AMP

You can grow in grace. As you live your life according to your spiritual DNA you can experience one grace, blessing, favor, and gift from Heaven after another. Can you sense God, in His graciousness, yearning to influence every area of your life? I'm not speaking of an emotional feeling but rather a spiritual recognition. God in His grace is calling and empowering you to grow in spiritual maturity and Christlikeness.

> *Therefore, laying aside all malice, all deceit, hypocrisy, envy, and all evil speaking, as newborn babes, desire the pure milk of the word, that you may grow thereby, if indeed you have tasted that the Lord is gracious.*
>
> 1 Peter 2:1-3

The Amplified Bible renders 1 Peter 2:1-3 as follows:

So be done with every trace of wickedness (depravity, malignity) and all deceit and insincerity (pretense, hypocrisy) and grudges (envy, jealousy) and slander and evil speaking of every kind.

Like newborn babies you should crave (thirst for, earnestly desire) the pure (unadulterated) spiritual milk, that by it you may be nurtured and grow unto [completed] salvation,

Since you have [already] tasted the goodness and kindness of the Lord.

We need to savor and partake of the graciousness, the goodness, and the kindness of the Lord. His grace is the nourishment and nutrition that satisfies every desire and need as we develop and mature in Him. Just like we need to have a balanced diet in terms of the food we eat, we need to have a balanced diet spiritually as well. Nutritionists tell us of the five major food groups. Perhaps we can think of these expressions of grace as the five major spiritual food groups:

- Saving Grace

- Sanctifying Grace

- Strengthening Grace

- Sharing Grace

- Serving Grace

"Oh, taste and see that the LORD is good" (Psalm 34:8)! If you partake of and grow in His grace you will be conformed more and more to the image and likeness of Jesus.

Chapter 6

WHAT GRACE IS NOT

Grace can neither be bought, earned, or won by the creature. If it could be, it would cease to be grace.

—Arthur W. Pink[1]

T he great sculptor Michelangelo said, "Every block of stone has a statue inside it, and it is the task of the sculptor to discover it. I saw the angel in the marble and carved until I set him free."[2] To uncover the true meaning of grace, then, we can also remove the concepts and perceptions of grace that are false or have nothing to do with God's grace—His spiritual DNA by which we live our lives.

1. The grace of God is not merely a prayer said before a meal.

It is good to give thanks for all of God's blessings, including your food (1 Timothy 4:3-4). There are several components in saying grace that are wonderful when heartfelt: gratitude, blessing, and thanksgiving, to name a few; and thanking God always reminds you of His grace toward you. However, His grace is far more than a simple prayer before eating.

2. The grace of God is not cultural sophistication or elegance.

A ballerina exhibits grace on the stage, and an etiquette book teaches social graces. Certain people are considered graceful or gracious, and these are wonderful traits. These may be appropriate usages of the English word, but God's grace involves so much more.

3. The grace of God is not the ability to miserably tolerate a situation.

On occasion, I have heard Christians bemoan the challenges they face. They complain, cry, or wallow in self-pity. Suddenly they blurt out, "But God is giving me grace," then continue in their misery. This is not God's grace! God's grace always inspires a note of faith and hope in our talk and our walk.

4. The grace of God is not a dead, theological concept.

God's grace is not a cerebrally stimulating theory; it is alive and powerful! Though we may attempt to understand God's grace intellectually, it is ultimately grasped with the heart. For example, imagine an individual who has studied every theory and fact regarding electricity and has received advanced degrees in electrical engineering. His bookshelves are lined with every book on the subject, but he lives in a shack with no electricity! He may know everything there is to know about electricity, but in his own personal life he is not experiencing any of its benefits.

We can theorize, speculate, debate, dissect, wax intellectual and philosophical, and study grace in multiple languages, but we will never receive God's transforming power of grace until we open our hearts to Him and His Word. Then God wants us to have more than knowledge of His grace; He wants us to be partakers of His grace.

5. The grace of God is not a passive attitude that God has toward us.

God is proactive about reaching us and blessing us, and there is nothing passive about His grace. Ephesians 1:7-8 gives us a picture of the active, pursuing nature of God's grace: "In Him we have redemption through His blood, the forgiveness of sins, according to the riches of His grace which He hath made to abound toward us in all wisdom and prudence."

Isn't that a glorious picture? God, in the riches of His grace and in His glorious generosity, has abounded toward us and lavished all of His grace, favor, and generosity on us! There is absolutely nothing passive, reluctant, or backward about the grace of God.

6. The grace of God is not a license to sin.

The book of Galatians is a battleground. Like a mighty general, Paul leads a truth invasion on the stranglehold of legalism that had assaulted the church in that region. Those who had begun walking with God in the glorious liberty of His grace had regressed and reverted back to a form of Mosaic legalism. As Paul contends for the grace of God, he says in Galatians 5:1: "Stand fast therefore in the liberty by which Christ has made us free, and do not be entangled again with a yoke of bondage." Paul also advises the Galatians to use their freedom properly. He tells them in verse 13: "For you, brethren, have been called to liberty; only do not use liberty as an opportunity for the flesh, but through love serve one another."

Throughout his epistles, Paul admonishes us that God's grace will always encourage us and enable us to resist temptation and sin. Following are just a few of the verses.

> *For the grace of God that brings salvation has appeared to all men, teaching us that, denying ungodliness and worldly lusts, we should live soberly, righteously, and godly in the present age.*
>
> Titus 2:11-12

> *Moreover the law entered that the offense might abound. But where sin abounded, grace abounded much more, so that as sin reigned in death, even so grace might reign through righteousness to eternal life through Jesus Christ our Lord.*
>
> *What shall we say then? Shall we continue in sin that grace may abound? Certainly not! How shall we who died to sin live any longer in it?*
>
> Romans 5:20-21; 6:1-2

7. The grace of God is not cheap.

Dietrich Bonhoeffer, the German pastor, theologian, and martyr, said: "Cheap grace is the preaching of forgiveness without requiring repentance, baptism without church discipline, communion without confession, absolution without personal confession. Cheap grace is grace without discipleship, grace without the Cross, grace without Jesus Christ, living and incarnate."[3]

Bonhoeffer used the term "cheap grace" to describe a diluted and distorted version of grace which he saw Christians handling casually and flippantly. He went on to describe the true grace of God, which he referred to as "costly grace."

It is costly because it condemns sin, and grace because it justifies the sinner. Above all, it is costly because it cost God the life of his Son: 'ye were bought at a price,' and what has cost God much cannot be cheap for us. Above all, it is grace because God did not reckon his Son too dear a price to pay for our life, but delivered him up for us. Costly grace is the Incarnation of God.[4]

Grace is costly. It is as sacred, holy, and as precious as the blood of Jesus that was shed for us. His grace, which permeates our spirit, should cause us to have reverence, awe, and respect for the God who so freely gave us such an extravagant gift.

8. The grace of God does not save us because of our performance.

Many people through the ages have said, "If I can just be good enough, God will love me and accept me." Such thinking makes man the initiator or performer and God the receiver, but God is always the giver and initiator.

And since it is through God's kindness, then it is not by their good works. For in that case, God's grace would not be what it really is—free and undeserved.

Romans 11:6 NLT

But if it is by grace (His unmerited favor and graciousness), it is no longer conditioned on works or anything men have done. Otherwise, grace would no longer be grace [it would be meaningless].

Romans 11:6 AMP

God's grace is the basis of our salvation, and thus we cannot take any glory for it. If we were somehow able to earn forgiveness, acceptance, and salvation, then we would deserve at least some of the credit. But if God gives them freely—totally separate from any work or behavior on our part—then He rightly deserves all the glory and honor.

Salvation is received by man, not achieved by man.

9. The grace of God is not an additive or a supplement to our salvation.

God's grace is the basic substance of our redemption. There is nothing supplemental about it. That's why I refer to God's grace as His DNA: it is the substance and essence of who He is and who He created us to be. This is why Paul told believers, "Put on your new nature, created to be like God—truly righteous and holy" (Ephesians 4:24 NLT).

Years ago I saw a Christian T-shirt that read, "Jesus adds life," a spin-off of a popular soft drink slogan. I was reminded of God's commandment in Deuteronomy 30:19 that His people "choose life." In the very next verse He said, "That you may love the LORD your God, that you may obey His voice, and that you may cling to Him, for He is your life and the length of your days" (Deuteronomy 30:20).

The grace of God through Jesus Christ is not an additive, supplement, or enhancement to our lives; He is our life.

10. The grace of God is not a cop-out from assuming responsibility or an excuse to avoid spiritual disciplines.

Grace is not a substitute; it is a catalyst. Grace does not replace other spiritual disciplines, it propels us into them. We need an ever-increasing awareness that grace is not only God's ability working toward us and in us, but also through us. When God gives us His ability and we respond accordingly, we have had a response to His ability: Hence, responsibility.

We should never minimize or underestimate the tendencies or the potential influence of our flesh. The flesh wants to be catered to, reign supreme, and is very happy to "cut corners" any way possible. I think that's why Paul said he disciplined his body and brought it under subjection (1 Corinthians 9:27). He also told believers that they were to, "kill (deaden, deprive of power) the evil desire lurking in your members [those animal impulses and all that is earthly in you that is employed in sin...]" (Colossians 3:5, AMP).

Some have grasped the reality that grace means they don't have to perform works in order to earn their salvation - and that is true. However, their flesh distorts and filters that message as, "I don't have to do anything. Period." They may end up abdicating and rebelling against many of the disciplines and expressions of obedience that followers of the Lord Jesus should embrace as their lives come into compliance with the Word of God. Believing that grace enables irresponsibility is a distortion and a deception. True grace is God's enablement, empowering us to respond to His ability and to His good plan for our lives.

11. Grace does not imply the absence of challenges or effort.

Jesus was full of grace, and the grace of God was upon Him, but He still faced intense challenges and pressures. The grace of God is what got Him through it all, without sin and without failure. Paul also faced severe opposition and learned the revolutionary lesson that God's grace was sufficient to sustain him and to see him through every difficulty.

Grace does not mean that we will not face challenges or ever have to fight. We do fight, but ours is the "...good fight of faith" (1 Timothy 6:12) because God's grace is mightily working in us and producing victory.

Chapter 7

THE MANIFOLD GRACE
OF GOD

It is God's mercy pitying, it is God's wisdom planning, it is God's power preparing, it is God's love providing.

—W. H. Griffith Thomas[1]

You may have heard about the group of blind men that were led to an elephant. Each of the men felt a different part, and then gave his respective description of an elephant.

- The man who felt the tail said an elephant was like a rope.

- The man who examined the leg said an elephant was like a tree.

- The man who held the trunk said an elephant was like a big water hose.

- The man who ran his hands over the side of the elephant said an elephant was like a wall.

- The man who felt an ear said an elephant was like a big, floppy leaf.

- The man who examined a tusk said an elephant was like a pipe.

Each of these men was correct in describing his encounter, but none of them provided a comprehensive description of an elephant. They may have argued over who was right, and in reality none of their descriptions were incorrect; however, each was incomplete. Only all of their accounts together would paint a true picture of the elephant.

This story is applicable to how we understand the grace of God.

- A person who was deep in sin and the bondages of the world prior to meeting Jesus might see God's grace as His delivering and rescuing power.

- A person who accepted the Lord at an early age and allowed the Word and the Spirit of God to govern his steps might see God's grace as an expression of His keeping power.

- A person who was called by God and was fulfilling a certain ministry might see God's grace as His enabling power.

- A person whose heart had been touched by God's comfort and strength during a time of great adversity would see God's grace as an expression of His sustaining power.

All of these would be accurate in their individual descriptions of how God's grace had blessed their lives. While each application or expression of grace was equally valid, grace was experienced differently by each person, potentially limiting their understanding of it. Like the blind men and the elephant, what each may think is grace in its totality is actually only a single expression of grace. One of the great challenges in defining the grace of God is that it is not narrow, constricted, or one-dimensional. As a matter of fact, the apostle Peter refers to "the manifold grace of God" (1 Peter 4:10).

Other Bible translations render that phrase:

- God's grace in its various forms (NIV)

- the varied grace of God (HCSB)

- God's various gifts of grace (NCV)

- God's many-sided kindness (WEY)

- the extremely diverse powers and gifts (AMP)
- the variegated grace of God (WUEST)

Peter's use of the word "manifold" indicates that God's grace is expressed in varied and diverse ways; it is truly multi-faceted. The word "manifold" originally meant "many folds." It was used in the 1800s to describe a musical instrument involving a "pipe or chamber with several outlets."[2]

A cut diamond with many facets also illustrates the meaning of manifold. As you turn the diamond, each facet will refract light differently and express a unique view of the gemstone. Yet, no matter which facet or group of facets you are viewing, in reality you are seeing the same diamond. In the same way, you miss so much if you hastily arrive at a single, simplistic definition of grace, and then look away. I would rather gaze long and admire the diamond of God's grace in order to see and appreciate every facet.

Manifold Electricity

Another illustration that helps us to more fully appreciate the manifold nature of God's grace is to consider the various applications of electricity. Imagine that a missionary friend of yours shows up at your house with some guests from a primitive tribe in another country. These people have never visited a modern community before, nor have they seen any type of modern convenience. As you open the door and welcome them, they see you flip a few wall switches and several lights come on. This amazes them, and with the missionary serving as an interpreter, they ask how that happened. Trying to keep it simple, you respond that the light bulbs shine because of electricity.

You notice it is a bit warm, so you hit another switch that turns on the ceiling fan. Your guests are fascinated with the motion producing the breeze and want to know how that happened. Again, you credit electricity.

Desiring to be hospitable, you invite your guests into the kitchen to offer them something to eat and drink. You can sense their curiosity, so you invite them over to the refrigerator. When you open it to get a drink, they are astonished to feel cold coming out of the big shiny box. Before they can even ask the question, you declare, "It's electricity."

You get some food out of the refrigerator and put it in the oven. When it is heated and you serve it to your guests, the foreigners are again astonished and curious. Once more you tell them that electricity is the source of the heat that warmed their food.

I think we can understand the bewilderment of your primitive guests. They are trying to comprehend how one force—electricity—can produce four totally different results: light, motion, cold, and heat. You and I understand that electricity will produce different results depending on what appliance it is serving. Electricity is power that can manifest in manifold ways.

Likewise, God's grace is manifold and can manifest in many ways. Depending on how we yield to, rely on, and cooperate with God, His grace will produce different results and have different expressions in our lives.

Scriptural Applications of Grace

To see the manifold grace of God, go back to Chapter 2, Grace in Scripture, and re-read the many applications and expressions of God's grace throughout the Bible. His grace accomplishes and produces wonderful results, and all to His glory! We can identify a few of the specific traits that the Bible associates with His grace:

- Grace is an integral part of who God is. The Father is gracious and He is the God of all grace. Jesus is full of grace, the grace of God is upon Him, and gracious words proceed out of His mouth. The Holy Spirit is the Spirit of Grace. Grace is God's DNA and the very fabric of His being.

- Such words as free, freely, gift, and given are associated with grace, as are salvation, saved, and justified.

- Additional actions and expressions of grace are indicated by other companion words and concepts, such as built up, enriched, help, empowered, established, strengthened, and growth.

Two things that stand out to me as I consider these facts:

1. Grace and graciousness pertain to God himself. We should not think of God's grace as an "it," as though it was some impersonal "thing" or commodity. Grace is God's nature and character emanating and flowing from His person and presence, the way light and heat emanate from the sun.

2. God's grace is active and productive. Whenever His grace is received, a variety of dynamic and powerful things happens. Tangible blessings are imparted into the lives of people, and lives are lifted, transformed, and empowered.

Questions for Reflection and Discussion:

- What was new and fresh about grace to you?

- What reinforced the understanding you already had of grace?

- What challenged your previous or current understanding of grace?

- Have you always seen God as a benevolent judge? How have you pictured Him through the years?

- How does the study of God's grace change your perception of who you are as His son or daughter?

- Is the role God's grace played in your initiation into the family of God different from the role His grace plays in your continuation in the family of God, as you walk with Him? Explain.

- Can grace be intellectually grasped or must it be experientially known? Explain.

- Why is *charis* such a difficult word for the religious mind to grasp ?

- Do you think there is good understanding of grace throughout the body of Christ? Why or why not?

- What do you think is the greatest misunderstanding about grace among unbelievers today? Among believers?

- With each facet of grace below, describe the work of God's grace in your life.

    - Saving grace is Love Rescuing.

    - Sanctifying grace is Love Cleansing.

    - Strengthening grace is Love Empowering.

    - Sharing grace is Love Supplying.

    - Serving grace is Love Assisting.

Part Three

WHAT IS
SAVING GRACE?

Chapter 8

THE BASICS

What! Get to Heaven on your own strength? Why, you might as well try to climb to the moon on a rope of sand!

—George Whitfield[1]

There is an old *Dennis the Menace* cartoon that wonderfully portrays grace. Dennis and his little buddy Joey are leaving the home of their kindly neighbor, Mrs. Wilson, cookies in hand. Joey asks Dennis, "I wonder what we did to deserve this?" Dennis then explains as only a child can. "Look Joey. Mrs. Wilson doesn't give us cookies because we're nice, but because she's nice."

If we can understand that simple cartoon, then we have a good beginning in understanding God's grace. The grace by which God saved us - which is even better than cookies - is based on His goodness, not on our performance or perfection. Our redemption was not an afterthought of God's either! It was His plan from eternity past.

...God, who has saved us and called us with a holy calling, not according to our works, but **according to His own purpose and grace** *which was given to us in Christ Jesus* **before time began.**

2 Timothy 1:8-9 (bold mine)

All who dwell on the earth will worship him,... **the Lamb slain from the foundation of the world.**

Revelation 13:8 (bold mine)

These scriptures reveal God's everlasting love and desire for us, so we can know without a doubt that there was nothing accidental about the grace of God being expressed to us through the offering of His Son. He has done and continues to do all things with our highest good in His mind and heart.

Saving grace is:

- God's power and ability to justify us, forgive our sins, and make us new creatures in Jesus Christ.

- God's power and ability that keeps us from being lost.

- The impartation of God's forgiveness.

- Love Rescuing.

Grace Is Unearned and Unmerited

We all had a need to be rescued from the catastrophic result of sin—eternal separation from God. The fact that this rescuing came by grace implies that there was something we could not achieve or accomplish by our own efforts. In short, we needed someone to do something for us that we could not accomplish for ourselves.

For God's redemption to truly be called grace, it had to be performed on the basis of His benevolence, goodwill, love, and generosity and not because He was obligated or indebted to us in any way. In other words, if He saved us because we had earned, merited, or deserved it, the help He provided would cease to be grace; it would simply fulfill a debt or an obligation.

The apostle Paul explains why all of humanity needs grace.

For everyone has sinned; we all fall short of God's glorious standard.

Romans 3:23 NLT

He later addresses the consequences of our sin, as well as God's response to our predicament.

For the wages of sin is death, but the free gift of God is eternal life through Christ Jesus our Lord.

Romans 6:23 NLT

Wages are what we earn or deserve based on our efforts and performance.

A **free gift** is something that is bestowed without cost to the recipient, as the giver has paid the price for it.

God saved you by his grace when you believed. And you can't take credit for this; it is a gift from God. Salvation is not a reward for the good things we have done, so none of us can boast about it.

Ephesians 2:8-9 NLT

The Amplified Bible renders this verse:

For it is by free grace (God's unmerited favor) that you are saved (delivered from judgment and made partakers of Christ's salvation) through [your] faith. And this [salvation] is not of yourselves [of your own doing, it came not through your own striving], but it is the gift of God;

Not because of works [not the fulfillment of the Law's demands], lest any man should boast. [It is not the result of what anyone can possibly do, so no one can pride himself in it or take glory to himself.]

Even though the Bible teaches this so clearly, many people (even in churches) still think that if they are good enough, do enough good works, or lead a good enough life, they will make it to Heaven. That may be popular religious thought, but it is not New Testament truth—and it negates the grace of God as the means of salvation.

God Is the Initiator

But God demonstrates His own love toward us, in that while we were
still sinners, Christ died for us.

Romans 5:8

God sent His Son to become a human being and physically demonstrate the Father's love and grace toward us. Through Jesus' life, death, and resurrection, God came for us—sinners all. L. E. Barton commented on just how deliberate and intentional God was in proactively pursuing us:

Grace therefore is the active, aggressive, militant (if you will) nature of God, combining all his mercy, love, and compassion and going on an endless quest for lost and ruined men.[2]

Grace is a free gift to us, but it cost Jesus His life. He did not wait for us to clean up our act, improve our attitude, show appreciation, straighten up, become perfect, or even show a sincere interest in God. When we were at our very worst, He gave us His very best. That is grace!

Paul mentioned the initiating nature of God's grace in Romans 10:20.

But Isaiah is very bold and says:
"I was found by those who did not seek Me;
I was made manifest to those who did not ask for Me."

John echoed this aspect of God's grace (His initiation of salvation) when he said,

This is real love—not that we loved God, but that he loved us and sent
his Son as a sacrifice to take away our sins.

1 John 4:10 NLT

Think about this. Before you had been born, had sinned, or had need of forgiveness, God had already made provision for your forgiveness and acceptance into His family. He provided a solution before you ever had a problem. Your own efforts, works, and performance could not save you, but Jesus' amazing sacrifice of love—shedding His precious blood, dying on the Cross, and being raised from the dead—made salvation available to you as a free gift. This is the essence of saving grace!

Grace is God reaching out to us when we were totally helpless to help ourselves. God paid a debt He did not owe (the penalty for our sin), so that we could receive gifts we could never earn (forgiveness, righteousness, and eternal life).

Try or Trust

The great scholar F. F. Bruce said,

Paul's claim [was] that the message he preached was the authentic gospel of Christ. It is this: two things on which Paul preeminently insisted—that salvation was provided by God's grace and that faith was the means by which men appropriated it.[3]

Remember the "wages of sin" and the "free gift of God." No one wants to receive the wages—what we deserve! But thank God for His free gift of saving grace.

When people work, their wages are not a gift, but something they have earned. But people are counted as righteous, not because of their work, but because of their faith in God who forgives sinners.

Romans 4:4-5 NLT

We have a very simple option when it comes to obtaining forgiveness and acceptance from God: We can try or we can trust. The Bible makes it very clear which option works and which one miserably fails. If our faith is in our "try," then we will get the wages we have earned (something we don't want). If our faith is in Him and what He has done—our "trust"—then we receive the wonderful gifts He freely extends.

Chapter 9

SAVED FROM WHAT?

Yes, it is wonderfully true that he does not count our sins against us. But it is not the ultimate wonder. The wonder of all wonders is that God counted our trespasses against his Son the Lord Jesus Christ. He did not pass them by; he punished them to the full in the person who "himself bore our sins in his body on the tree" (1 Peter 2:24).

—Sinclair B. Ferguson[1]

Words such as "saved" and "salvation" are used so frequently, casually, and flippantly that I wonder if we sometimes fail to appreciate their true value and significance. Jesus didn't come into this world to save us from having a bad hair day, to simply give us a positive attitude, to merely improve our lives, or to rescue us from some minor inconveniences. He didn't come only to make us happy, successful, or fulfilled.

Certainly, these are some of the many secondary and peripheral benefits to being in relationship with God through Jesus Christ, but the driving and compelling purpose in Jesus coming to this Earth was to save humanity—us—from sin, from our separation from God, from our lostness. In a sense, He came to save us from our fallen selves.

God Is Just

O Israel, thou hast destroyed thyself; but in me is thine help.

Hosea 13:9 KJV

Your iniquities have separated you from your God;

And your sins have hidden His face from you.

Isaiah 59:2

We really needed help, and help us He did! He sent Jesus to the Cross. There are those who think the Cross was unnecessary. They are sadly mistaken. Paul referred to "the offense of the cross" (Galatians 5:11) and said, "The message of the cross is foolishness to those who are perishing, but to us who are being saved it is the power of God" (1 Corinthians 1:18). How is such a seemingly cruel act—the crucifixion of the Son of God—the power of God? It paid the full debt of mankind's sin.

Perhaps some think God looks the other way or ignores the sins of humanity because He is a God of love. However, the Bible also teaches that God is just. Deuteronomy 32:4 says,

All His ways are justice,

A God of truth and without injustice;

Righteous and upright is He.

Stop and think about this for a moment. What would we say of an earthly judge who dismissed every case brought before him in spite of massive, incriminating evidence against the accused, even in heinous crimes? What if he chose to overlook every criminal act that was presented to him? We would say that such a judge was corrupt and did not uphold justice. We would rightly be concerned that the message such irresponsible leniency would be sending to our society is: Crime is okay and has no consequences.

There is absolutely nothing in the Bible—including God's grace—that indicates God is light on sin. Consider the following:

- "The LORD God…by no means clearing the guilty" (Exodus 34:6-7).

- "A just God and a Savior" (Isaiah 45:21).

- "Every one shall die for his own iniquity" (Jeremiah 31:30).

- "He reserves wrath for His enemies" (Nahum 1:2).

- God is "of purer eyes than to behold evil" and He "cannot look on wickedness" (Habakkuk 1:13).

Even when we move into the New Testament, we find God still hates sin and is just. Paul said that those who were stubborn and refused to repent from sin and be saved were, "storing up terrible punishment" for themselves, and that, "a day of anger is coming, when God's righteous judgment will be revealed" (Romans 2:5 NLT).

When the Lord Jesus is revealed from heaven with His mighty angels, in flaming fire taking vengeance on those who do not know God, and on those who do not obey the gospel of our Lord Jesus Christ. These shall be punished with everlasting destruction from the presence of the Lord.

2 Thessalonians 1:7-9

Of Jesus, Scripture says, "You have loved righteousness and hated lawlessness" (Hebrews 1:9). Hebrews 10:31 goes on to say, "It is a fearful thing to fall into the hands of the living God," and Hebrews 12:29 says, "Our God is a consuming fire." What should we do then? Jude said, "Rescue others by snatching them from the flames of judgment" (Jude 23 NLT).

Jesus said that He hated both the deeds and the doctrine of a group called the Nicolaitans (Revelation 2:6,15). They were a sect believed to be founded by Nicolas, one of the seven deacons appointed to wait on tables in Acts 6. Nicolas taught that because Christians were no longer under the Law, they were free to live as they pleased. They could participate in pagan festivals, which involved idolatry and immorality, and engage in any type of behavior they desired. It was a perversion of the gospel and the biblical doctrine of grace.

In addition to the glories of Heaven described in the book of Revelation, there is also a stark description of final judgment, which will take place at the Great White Throne.

And anyone not found written in the Book of Life was cast into the lake of fire.

Revelation 20:15

Hell is Real

Some have tried to reason away Hell. Those who reject the authority of the Bible may say that Hell is simply a result of man's imagination. Some who use the Bible to support their unbiblical opinions acknowledge that Hell is taught in the Bible, but they believe no one will go to Hell because Jesus died for everyone's sins, which means everyone will be forgiven and go to Heaven. This latter idea is often referred to as universalism or ultimate reconciliation.

I'm not against using reason, but we were never meant to exalt our own reasoning above the Word of God. God invited us to reason with Him not against Him, and His reasoning is found in the Bible.

"Come now, and let us reason together,"
Says the LORD,
"Though your sins are like scarlet,
They shall be as white as snow;
Though they are red like crimson,
They shall be as wool."

Isaiah 1:18

Recognizing how difficult it is for us to accept the horrendous reality of Hell, C. S. Lewis said,

> There is no doctrine which I would more willingly remove from Christianity than the doctrine of Hell, if it lay in my power. But it has the full support of Scripture and, especially, of our Lord's own words; it has always been held by the Christian Church, and it has the support of reason.[2]

To embrace the idea that everyone will automatically be saved based upon Jesus' death, one would have to completely disregard the numerous scriptures that plainly teach salvation and forgiveness must be received by faith by the individual. For example, John 1:12 says, "But as many as received Him, to them He gave the right to become children of God, to those who believe in His name."

William Evans skillfully pointed out the difference between what God has made available as opposed to what man actually receives:

> The atonement is sufficient for all; it is efficient for those who believe in Christ. The atonement itself, so far as it lays the basis for the redemptive dealing of God with men is unlimited; the application of the atonement is limited to those who actually believe in Christ. He is the Savior of all men potentially (1 Timothy 1:15); of believers alone effectually (1 Timothy 4:10). "For therefore we both labor and suffer reproach, because we believe in the living God, who is the Saviour of men, specially of those that believe." The atonement is limited only by men's unbelief.[3]

We should never address such a weighty topic as Hell and eternal damnation lightly. D. L. Moody said, "I cannot preach on hell unless I preach with tears."[4] And Paul said, "Knowing, therefore, the terror of the Lord, we persuade men" (2 Corinthians 5:11).

Jesus Was Born to Save

Grace does not mean God excuses sin. Paul encouraged us to consider both the goodness and the severity of God (Romans 11:22). Having received His grace, we get to enjoy His goodness, but make no mistake about it—God still hates sin. The Good News is that even though God abhors sin, He loves us; and that is why He sent Jesus to save us from our sins and restore us to Himself.

- The angel Gabriel told Joseph, "And she [Mary] will bring forth a Son, and you shall call His name Jesus, for He will save His people from their sins" (Matthew 1:21, brackets mine).

- Jesus said of Himself, "The Son of Man has come to seek and to save that which was lost" (Luke 19:10).

- Paul said, "This is a faithful saying and worthy of all acceptance, that Christ Jesus came into the world to save sinners, of whom I am chief" (1 Timothy 1:15).

- After Jesus had purchased salvation for us, Peter told those listening to him, "Be saved from this perverse generation" (Acts 2:40).

- Paul said of the salvation we have through Jesus, "Much more then, having now been justified by His blood, we shall be saved from wrath through Him" (Romans 5:9). He reinforced this thought when he said, "For God did not appoint us to wrath, but to obtain salvation through our Lord Jesus Christ" (1 Thessalonians 5:9).

For God did not send His Son into the world to condemn the world, but that the world through Him might be saved.

He who believes in Him is not condemned; but he who does not believe is condemned already, because he has not believed in the name of the only begotten Son of God.

John 3:17-18

What we do see is Jesus, who was given a position "a little lower than the angels"; and because he suffered death for us, he is now "crowned with glory and honor." Yes, by God's grace, Jesus tasted death for everyone.

Hebrews 2:9 NLT

What an amazing thought! Jesus Christ, our perfect and sinless substitute, tasted death for everyone. The Bible even says how He did it: by God's grace. It was God's love, compassion, and mercy for you and for me that not only sent Jesus to the Cross but enabled Him to endure it. Jesus was no helpless victim of hatred or persecution. He voluntarily surrendered Himself to death.

"No one takes it from Me, but I lay it down of Myself. I have power to lay it down, and I have power to take it again."

John 10:18

Jesus went to the Cross willingly, knowing that Isaiah 53:6 was going to be fulfilled as He suffered on our behalf:

All we like sheep have gone astray;
We have turned, every one, to his own way;
And the LORD has laid on Him the iniquity of us all.

As our substitute on the Cross, Jesus suffered the unimaginable and the incomprehensible. Grace never means that God is light on sin! Grace means God placed sin and the punishment for sin on His only Son so we would never have to incur His wrath. First Thessalonians 5:9 says, "God did not appoint us to wrath, but to obtain salvation through our Lord Jesus Christ." What was the basis for this?

Therefore, if anyone is in Christ, he is a new creation; old things have passed away; behold, all things have become new. Now all things are of God, who has reconciled us to Himself through Jesus Christ, and has given us the ministry of reconciliation, that is, that God was in Christ reconciling the world to Himself, **not imputing their trespasses to them,** *and has committed to us the word of reconciliation.*

For He made Him who knew no sin to be sin for us, that we might become the righteousness of God in Him.

2 Corinthians 5:17-19,21 (bold mine)

For you know the grace of our Lord Jesus Christ, that though He was rich, yet for your sakes He became poor, that you through His poverty might become rich.

2 Corinthians 8:9

Christ has redeemed us from the curse of the law, having become a curse for us (for it is written, "Cursed is everyone who hangs on a tree"), that the blessing of Abraham might come upon the Gentiles in Christ Jesus, that we might receive the promise of the Spirit through faith.

Galatians 3:13-14

Remember, it was by grace that He tasted death for every man, woman, and child. It was by grace that the sins of the world were laid upon Him, that He was made poor for us, and that He was made a curse for us. It is also by grace that God makes us righteous, enriches our lives, and blesses us. It was the grace of God working in and through Jesus that motivated everything He did for us.

The Gravity of Sin and the Greatness of His Love

John Chrysostom, who became Archbishop of Constantinople in 398 A.D., said, "By the Cross we know the gravity of sin and the greatness of God's love towards us."[5] It is common, and rightly so, that we hear much about the love of God. However, it is also important to understand what Chrysostom referred to as "the gravity of sin." Noted Bible commentator Harry Ironside said,

> No finite mind can fathom the depths of woe and anguish into which the soul of Jesus sank when that dread darkness spread o'er all the scene.
>
> It was a symbol of the spiritual darkness into which He went as the Man Christ Jesus made sin for us that we might become the righteousness of God in Him.
>
> It was then that God laid on Him the iniquity of us all that His soul was made an offering for sin. We get some faint understanding of what this meant for Him when, just as the darkness was passing, we hear Him cry, "My God, My God, why hast Thou forsaken Me?" Each believer can reply, "It was that I might never be forsaken." He took our place and endured the wrath of God our sins deserved. This was the cup from which he shrank in Gethsemane; now, pressed to His lips, He drained it to the dregs.[6]

Ironside further expounded on the sufferings of Christ in a sermon entitled "The Sinless One Made Sin":

> In some way our finite minds can not now understand, the pent-up wrath of the centuries fell upon Him, and He sank in deep mire where there was no standing, as He endured in His inmost being what you and I would have had to endure through all eternity, had it not been for His mighty sacrifice.[7]

When we catch a glimpse of the sufferings of Christ on the Cross and understand that the precious blood of the sinless, spotless Son of God was shed on our behalf (Hebrews 9:22), then we can begin to grasp what Ephesians 3:18 MSG describes as "the extravagant dimensions of Christ's love." This grace—the grace by which Christ tasted death for everyone—demonstrates the magnificence of the love God has for us. It is not a theoretical love or a philosophical love; it is a love demonstrated in the most intentional of actions. Under the gravity of our sin, Jesus died for us.

> *And you He made alive, who were dead in trespasses and sins,...we all once conducted ourselves in the lusts of our flesh, fulfilling the desires of the flesh and of the mind, and were by nature children of wrath, just as the others.*
>
> *But God, who is rich in mercy, because of His great love with which He loved us, even when we were dead in trespasses, made us alive together with Christ (by grace you have been saved).*
>
> Ephesians 2:1,3-5

Through the grace of God, Jesus saved us from sin, a formerly corrupt life, eternal separation from God, wrath, spiritual death, and Hell. The salvation that has come to us through the grace and the goodness of God is no small thing. Neither was this grace acquired cheaply. Grace may be free to us, but it cost Jesus His blood and His life. That is why we must never treat His grace lightly or disrespectfully.

In His great grace, God purposed that His own Son Jesus would take the punishment and penalty that our sin deserved so that we could be forgiven. It's not that judgment no longer exists; it does. But Jesus took our place, and we are now free. Spurgeon expressed it so well when he said, "Justice is honored, and law is vindicated in the sacrifice of Christ. Since God is satisfied, I may well be so."[8]

Chapter 10

BUT I'M A LAW-ABIDING CITIZEN!

The Law tells me how crooked I am. Grace comes along and straightens me out.

—D.L. Moody[1]

I grew up in church and remember hearing the Ten Commandments at a fairly young age. However, before I became old enough to understand what they meant, I had already violated some of them.

- Before I knew what "Thou Shalt Not Covet" meant, I had already coveted a piece of candy my brother had.

- Before I knew what "Thou Shalt Not Steal" meant, I had already taken his piece of candy when he wasn't looking.

- Before I knew what "Thou Shalt Not Lie" meant, I had already denied taking that piece of candy when my mom asked me about it.

The law is "holy and right and good" (Romans 7:12 NLT). The problem is that I wasn't. This is why it is futile for any person to think that he or she is going to be right with God based on his or her own works or performance.

It is amazing though, to realize how many people think they can make it to Heaven because they are a relatively good person. Perhaps they compare themselves to others whom they feel are worse than they are. Or maybe they believe that because they have kept most of the Ten Commandments most of the time, they will be okay.

It is extremely important to understand that none of us are going to make it to Heaven because we have been law-abiding citizens. Heaven is not for good people, perfect people, or religious people. Heaven is for people who have been forgiven. And forgiveness is available because of what Jesus has done for us. We can never be good enough, perfect enough, or religious enough to earn Heaven on our own. We must rely completely on the work of Jesus.

The Law Points to Jesus

When Christians hear the term "Law," they typically think of the Ten Commandments God gave to the nation of Israel through Moses (Exodus 20:2-17; Deuteronomy 5:6-21). A concise, condensed summary of these commandments is as follows:

1. You shall have no other gods before Me.
2. You shall not make for yourself a carved image.
3. You shall not take the name of the Lord your God in vain.
4. Remember the Sabbath day, to keep it holy.
5. Honor your father and your mother.
6. You shall not murder.
7. You shall not commit adultery.
8. You shall not steal.
9. You shall not bear false witness against your neighbor.
10. You shall not covet.

The first four commandments pertain to our responsibilities toward God, while the last six deal with our responsibilities to our fellow human beings. Jesus recognized both aspects when He was asked which commandment in the Law was the greatest.

> *Jesus said to him, "'You shall love the LORD your God with all your heart, with all your soul, and with all your mind.' This is the first and great commandment. And the second is like it: 'You shall love your neighbor as yourself.' On these two commandments hang all the Law and the Prophets."*
>
> Matthew 22:37-40

After giving the Ten Commandments, God told Moses He was going to give him even more commandments, and that he was to teach these to the people.

> *"Therefore you shall be careful to do as the LORD your God has commanded you; you shall not turn aside to the right hand or to the left. You shall walk in all the ways which the LORD your God has commanded you, that you may live and that it may be well with you, and that you may prolong your days in the land which you shall possess."*
>
> Deuteronomy 5:32-33

God wanted things to go favorably for His people, and if you stop and think about it, any society that would embrace the values communicated in the Ten Commandments would certainly be a better, healthier, and safer society to live in than one that would reject them. There are significant civil and domestic benefits associated with respecting and obeying the commandments of God.

While the Ten Commandments may be the most well known of Old Testament laws, there were actually hundreds of other laws given. Those who have counted them (and I have not) tell us there are a total of 613 Old Testament laws. It is also said that there are 248 positive (thou shalt) commandments and 365 negative (thou shalt not) commandments.

Beyond those laws articulated in the Old Testament, rabbis regularly added commentaries, interpretations, and applications to these hundreds of laws, creating even more rules and traditions. No doubt many of these individuals were devout, God-fearing men who esteemed God and His Word greatly. However, by the time Jesus came on the scene, some who specialized in the intricacies of "the letter of the Law" had become religious bullies. Jesus' harshest rebukes were reserved for such legalists. Here is just some of what He had to say:

> *Then Jesus said to the crowds and to his disciples, "The teachers of religious law and the Pharisees are the official interpreters of the law of Moses. So practice and obey whatever they tell you, but don't follow their example. For they don't practice what they teach. They crush people with unbearable religious demands and never lift a finger to ease the burden.*
>
> *"Everything they do is for show. On their arms they wear extra wide prayer boxes with Scripture verses inside, and they wear robes with extra long tassels."*
>
> Matthew 23:1-5 NLT

Jesus indicated that their pride, their lack of compassion for others, and their nit-picky focus on minutiae had caused them to miss the most important aspects of the Law: justice, mercy, and faith (Matthew 23:23). In John 5:39-40 NLT, Jesus said they had missed seeing something else that is very important in Scripture: Him.

> *"You search the Scriptures because you think they give you eternal life. But the Scriptures point to me! Yet you refuse to come to me to receive this life."*

Had their eyes been opened, they would have seen that beyond the domestic and civil benefits of the Old Testament Law, its ultimate purpose was to point and direct them to Jesus. Jesus had not come to destroy the Law but to fulfill it.

"Don't misunderstand why I have come. I did not come to abolish the law of Moses or the writings of the prophets. No, I came to accomplish their purpose."

Matthew 5:17 NLT

After His resurrection, Jesus had a conversation with two of His disciples, attempting to open their eyes to see Him in the Old Testament Law and the Prophets.

And beginning at Moses and all the Prophets, He expounded to them in all the Scriptures the things concerning Himself.

Luke 24:27

The entire Old Testament had been preparation for the coming of Jesus to carry out God's plan of redeeming mankind unto Himself.

Paul's ministry carried the same message. When he arrived in Rome, Acts 28:23 says that Paul spent an entire day with Jewish leaders, "to whom he explained and solemnly testified of the kingdom of God, persuading them concerning Jesus from both the Law of Moses and the Prophets, from morning till evening." Why did Jesus and the apostles stress the Law? The Law enabled people to see their sin; and this helps them realize their need for a savior.

The Purpose of the Law

The law was given through Moses, but grace and truth came through Jesus Christ.

John 1:17

Study in the New Testament brings clarification to the distinction between the Law and grace, especially in the writings of Paul. In Galatians 3:18 NLT, he explains that the inheritance God has for His people cannot be received based upon their keeping the Law, but rather, "God graciously gave it to Abraham as a promise." If the Law was incapable of "delivering the goods" to people, then why did God give the Law in the first place? Paul asks the same question:

Why, then, was the law given? It was given alongside the promise to show people their sins. But the law was designed to last only until the coming of the child who was promised.

Is there a conflict, then, between God's law and God's promises? Absolutely not! If the law could give us new life, we could be made right with God by obeying it. But the Scriptures declare that we are all prisoners of sin, so we receive God's promise of freedom only by believing in Jesus Christ.

Before the way of faith in Christ was available to us, we were placed under guard by the law. We were kept in protective custody, so to speak, until the way of faith was revealed.

Let me put it another way. The law was our guardian until Christ came; it protected us until we could be made right with God through faith. And now that the way of faith has come, we no longer need the law as our guardian.

Galatians 3:19,21-25 NLT

In answering why God gave the Law, Paul made these points:

- The Law was given to show people their sins (verse 19).

- The Law was temporary and only designed to last "until the coming of the child who was promised," Jesus (verse 19).

- The Law could not give us new life (verse 21).

- Apart from Christ, all mankind are prisoners of sin (verse 22).

- The Law was our tutor to bring us to Christ, that we might be "justified by faith" (verse 24 NKJV).

- The Law was a guardian (or a form of protective custody) until people had the opportunity to be made right with God through faith (verses 23-24).

- Now that the way of faith has come, we no longer need the Law as our guardian (verse 25).

Before we can understand and fully appreciate how God's grace saves us, it is good to understand why the Law could not.

- The Law was never given to save us, but to show us we needed salvation.

- The Law was never given to make us righteous, but to show us we were unrighteous.

- The Law was never given to justify us, but to show us we needed justification.

Before we will seek or be open to receive help, we have to realize and accept that we need help. The Law of God, in no uncertain terms, reveals to us that we have sinned and fallen short of God's holy standard.

Obviously, the law applies to those to whom it was given, for its purpose is to keep people from having excuses, and to show that the entire world is guilty before God. For no one can ever be made right with God by doing what the law commands. The law simply shows us how sinful we are.

Romans 3:19-20 NLT

To put it another way, the Law was a ten-foot measuring stick to show us that we are only five or six feet tall, a straight edge to show us how crooked we are, and a mirror to show us where our faults are. Our natural inclination might be to think that if the Law points out our sins and problems, then it must be a bad thing. On the contrary, the Law is good. Paul said, "The law is good when used correctly" (1 Timothy 1:8 NLT).

Imagine you have enjoyed a meal with some friends and are getting ready to leave the restaurant. If one of your friends mentions that you have spaghetti sauce on your chin, does that make your friend a bad person? In reality, that person is doing you a favor even though it may embarrass you for a moment.

What if you were eating by yourself, go into the restroom, and in the mirror you see you have sauce on your chin. Is the mirror a bad thing because it enabled you to see your problem? Should you get mad at the mirror and break it? Of course not. The problem is not with the mirror; the problem is with you. Even though the mirror seems to be making you look bad, it is really revealing a problem you need to know about. Only an unwise person would blame the mirror.

However, that mirror has limitations. It can only show you where the sauce is; it cannot clean the sauce off your chin. Likewise, the Law that came through Moses reveals your sin, but it cannot remove your sin. The Law is the schoolmaster who teaches you where you have missed it. You need a savior. That's where Jesus comes in with grace and truth. We know Paul had this very experience because he wrote,

It was the law that showed me my sin. I would never have known that coveting is wrong if the law had not said, "You must not covet."

Romans 7:7 NLT

The Law itself is good, but it revealed something in us that was not good. The problem was not with the Law; the problem was with us. The Law did not create the problem; it simply revealed the problem that was intrinsic in our fallen nature and had manifested through our sinful behavior (thoughts, words, and deeds). The Law revealed the problem; Jesus is our solution!

The Galatian Problem

The book of Galatians deals extensively with salvation and trusting Christ. Great tension surfaces in this book because legalistic teachers were telling the Galatians that salvation was a matter of Christ plus: Christ plus circumcision or Christ plus keeping the Law. In other words, a person was saved by Jesus' blood and their own works. These teachers were not rejecting Christ outright, but they were undermining the sufficiency of His redemptive work by saying salvation was achieved by accepting Christ plus something else instead of being fully received through accepting Christ alone.

Today's legalists might say salvation is obtained by Christ plus obeying the Ten Commandments, Christ plus church attendance, or Christ plus doing good works. But grace and faith still declare that salvation is by faith in Christ—period! There is nothing "plus" about it!

Keeping the Ten Commandments, attending church, and doing good works are all wonderful, but they are not how we are saved. Paul says, "But if it is by grace, it is no longer on the basis of works, otherwise grace is no longer grace" (Romans 11:6 NASBU). In 1892 Rudyard Kipling wrote, "East is East, and West is West, and never the twain shall meet." In light of Romans 11:6, I say, "Grace is Grace and Works are Works, and never the twain shall meet."

Just How Good Would You Have to Be?

Anyone who tries to live by his own effort, independent of God, is doomed to failure. Scripture backs this up: "Utterly cursed is every person who fails to carry out every detail written in the Book of the law."

Galatians 3:10 MSG

The person who keeps all of the laws except one is as guilty as a person who has broken all of God's laws.

James 2:10 NLT

The only passing grade with God is 100 percent, which none of us are capable of earning. We have all sinned and fallen short (Romans 3:23), but Jesus never did. God's grace gives us Jesus' score on our "report card" the moment we trust in Him alone for our salvation. This is why the gospel is Good News! In Jesus Christ we obtain a perfect score, are completely forgiven of our sins, and are granted eternal life with Him in Heaven.

Not only did Paul and James recognize the inability of the Law to save us from sin, but Peter did as well. In Acts 15, a conference was held in Jerusalem to discuss whether Gentiles needed to be circumcised and keep the Law in order to be true followers of the Lord. Peter challenged those who wanted to put Gentiles under the Law with these words:

"So why are you now challenging God by burdening the Gentile believers with a yoke that neither we nor our ancestors were able to bear? We believe that we are all saved the same way, by the undeserved grace of the Lord Jesus."

Acts 15:10-11 NLT

Note the two points that Peter makes:

- The Old Testament law was a burdensome yoke they had not been able to keep.

- There is only one way in which all people—Jews and Gentiles alike—obtain salvation: through the grace of the Lord Jesus Christ.

The law was without power, because the law was made weak by our sinful selves. But God did what the law could not do. He sent his own Son to earth with the same human life that others use for sin. By sending his Son to be an offering for sin, God used a human life to destroy sin. He did this so that we could be the kind of people the law correctly wants us to be. Now we do not live following our sinful selves, but we live following the Spirit.

Romans 8:3-4 NCV

The Law fails to bring forgiveness and salvation to us because it was never designed to do that. God gave the Law to show us we need forgiveness and salvation; and in that it is an unparalleled success.

But now God has shown us a way to be made right with him without keeping the requirements of the law, as was promised in the writings of Moses and the prophets long ago. We are made right with God by placing our faith in Jesus Christ. And this is true for everyone who believes, no matter who we are.

For everyone has sinned; we all fall short of God's glorious standard. Yet God, with undeserved kindness, declares that we are righteous. He did this through Christ Jesus when he freed us from the penalty for our sins. For God presented Jesus as the sacrifice for sin. People are made right with God when they believe that Jesus sacrificed his life, shedding his blood. This sacrifice shows that God was being fair when he held back and did not punish those who sinned in times past, for he was looking ahead and including them in what he would do in this present time. God did this to demonstrate his righteousness, for he himself is fair and just, and he declares sinners to be right in his sight when they believe in Jesus.

Can we boast, then, that we have done anything to be accepted by God? No, because our acquittal is not based on obeying the law. It is based on faith. So we are made right with God through faith and not by obeying the law.

Romans 3:21-28 NLT

In the passage above we see four powerful positive truths about the effects of God's grace.

- We are made right with God by faith in Him (verse 22).

- God declares we are righteous (verse 24).

- God frees us from the penalty of our sins (verse 24).

- God declares sinners to be right in His sight when they believe in Jesus (verse 26).

This is Good News for you and me. Don't get so caught up in your past failures that you neglect what God's grace brought you to: A new life in Jesus Christ! Emphasize what the Bible emphasizes: God's grace is greater than the Law that revealed your sin and the sin that it revealed. His grace has birthed you into His family and made you His child whom He cherishes.

Never forget that you were lost without Him, but thank God you are no longer without Him! You can rejoice that through His grace He has given you a new beginning, a new destiny, and a new identity in Christ.

Chaper 11

FROM SHADOW TO SUBSTANCE

The law works fear and wrath; grace works hope and mercy.
—Martin Luther[1]

W e now know the perfect moral standard of the Law, which exposes our sinful nature and helps us realize that we need a savior. The Law also has a ceremonial or ritualistic side that also points to Jesus the Messiah. You might already be aware that the Old Testament describes the frequent sacrifice of animals. Such sacrifices were performed long before God gave the Law, but they were eventually regulated by the Law. The New Testament reveals that those sacrifices were instituted to paint a prophetic picture that pointed to Jesus as the ultimate and final sacrifice for the sins of mankind.

When John the Baptist introduced Jesus to the people, he said, "Behold! The Lamb of God who takes away the sin of the world!" (John 1:29). Peter later wrote, "You know that God paid a ransom to save you from the empty life you inherited from your ancestors. And the ransom he paid was not mere gold or silver. It was the precious blood of Christ, the sinless, spotless Lamb of God" (1 Peter 1:18-19 NLT). And in the book of Revelation, John describes Jesus as a lamb twenty-six times.

What a powerful statement! John the Baptist and the apostles were saying, "Jesus is the true Lamb, the one foreshadowed throughout the Old Testament, He is the One who has been slain for our sins."

While the book of Romans reveals the inadequacy of the Law to save us from our sins and keep us from sinning after we are saved, the book of Hebrews reveals the inadequacy of the Law's ceremonies and sacrifices to save and keep us from sinning. However, Romans and Hebrews make the same point: The Law, the feasts, and the sacrifices were all designed to point to, reveal, and describe the coming Messiah. The feasts and sacrifices were types, shadows, and symbols, or what we might call prophetic pictures of redemption and the Son of God who would accomplish it.

Shadow and Substance

In Colossians, Paul refers to certain Old Testament events like holy days, new moon ceremonies, and Sabbaths as "a shadow of things to come, but the substance is of Christ" (Colossians 2:17). Hebrews 8:5 NLT tells us that the High Priest of the Old Testament served, "in a system of worship that is only a copy, a shadow of the real one in heaven."

> *The old system under the law of Moses was only a shadow, a dim preview of the good things to come, not the good things themselves. The sacrifices under that system were repeated again and again, year after year, but they were never able to provide perfect cleansing for those who came to worship. If they could have provided perfect cleansing, the sacrifices would have stopped, for the worshipers would have been purified once for all time, and their feelings of guilt would have disappeared.*
>
> *But instead, those sacrifices actually reminded them of their sins year after year. For it is not possible for the blood of bulls and goats to take away sins.*
>
> Hebrews 10:1-4 NLT

Stop and think about what a shadow is. If you are standing in the middle of a field, and an airplane is flying overhead, you might see its shadow on the ground racing toward you. Even though the shadow is the shape of the plane, you are not afraid the shadow will hit you because you know it has no substance. Furthermore, you cannot get in the shadow of a plane and go anywhere because it has no substance. However, the shadow tells you that a tangible, real airplane exists and is flying overhead.

Consider the shadow cast by a glass of water. You may be able to tell that the shadow is that of a glass of water, but that shadow could never satisfy your thirst. It can only tell you that somewhere close by there is a real glass of water. The shadow gives you an image of the substance, but it has no substance itself. Likewise, the Old Testament feasts, traditions, and sacrifices could not actually save people from sin. They could only point toward the One casting the shadow—the Lord Jesus Christ—the One who would ultimately come as the true Lamb of God to take away the sin of the world.

Hebrews Nails it Down

Hebrews, chapter 7, addresses the difference between the Aaronic priesthood, which is associated with the Law of Moses, and the priesthood of Melchizedek, which foreshadowed the priesthood of Jesus.

> *The old requirement about the priesthood was set aside because it was weak and useless. For the law never made anything perfect. But now we have confidence in a better hope, through which we draw near to God.*
>
> Hebrews 7:18-19 NLT

> *But because Jesus lives forever, his priesthood lasts forever. Therefore he is able, once and forever, to save those who come to God through him. He lives forever to intercede with God on their behalf.*

He is the kind of high priest we need because he is holy and blameless, unstained by sin. He has been set apart from sinners and has been given the highest place of honor in heaven. Unlike those other high priests, he does not need to offer sacrifices every day. They did this for their own sins first and then for the sins of the people. But Jesus did this once for all when he offered himself as the sacrifice for the people's sins.

Hebrews 7:24-27 NLT

The Old Testament priesthood was set aside, and Jesus' priesthood endures forever! What the other priests did symbolically, offering lambs, bulls, goats, and other sacrifices, Jesus did substantively by offering Himself. Hebrews, chapter 8, goes on to elaborate on this "changing of the guard."

They serve in a system of worship that is only a copy, a shadow of the real one in heaven. For when Moses was getting ready to build the Tabernacle, God gave him this warning: "Be sure that you make everything according to the pattern I have shown you here on the mountain."

But now Jesus, our High Priest, has been given a ministry that is far superior to the old priesthood, for he is the one who mediates for us a far better covenant with God, based on better promises.

If the first covenant had been faultless, there would have been no need for a second covenant to replace it. But when God found fault with the people, he said:

"The day is coming, says the LORD, when I will make a new covenant with the people of Israel and Judah."

Hebrews 8:5-8 NLT

Paul points out that the first covenant had to be replaced because there was a fault. It was not the fault of the Law itself, but the fault was with us. The Law merely revealed our fault.

The old system under the law of Moses was only a shadow, a dim pre-view of the good things to come, not the good things themselves. The sacrifices under that system were repeated again and again, year after year, but they were never able to provide perfect cleansing for those who came to worship. If they could have provided perfect cleansing, the sacrifices would have stopped, for the worshipers would have been purified once for all time, and their feelings of guilt would have disap-peared.

But instead, those sacrifices actually reminded them of their sins year after year. For it is not possible for the blood of bulls and goats to take away sins.

Then he [Christ] said, "Look, I have come to do your will." He cancels the first covenant in order to put the second into effect.

But our High Priest offered himself to God as a single sacrifice for sins, good for all time. Then he sat down in the place of honor at God's right hand.

For by that one offering he forever made perfect those who are being made holy.

And when sins have been forgiven, there is no need to offer any more sacrifices.

Hebrews 10:1-4,9,12,14,18 NLT

We have seen why the Law was unable to save us. Not only could we not measure up to its standards, but its sacrifices and feasts were mere shadows of the substance that was to come in the person of Jesus.

Gentiles and the Law

At this point you might be asking, "Why all this discussion of the Law? I'm not Jewish." In reality, the average 21st century believer never "kept the law" that Paul spoke of, nor was there an attempt to do so. To this very day, most believers don't have a clue as to what the majority of the 613 Old Testament laws even were. When people say that before they were born again they were "under the law," what they usually mean is that they acknowledged that the Ten Commandments were God's authoritative standard of right living and that they tried to obey them. But that's just a minute fraction of what Paul was referring to when he said "...concerning the righteousness which is in the law," that he was "blameless" (Philippians 3:6).

A Pharisee like Paul would have found it humorous if we thought that a Gentile being under the Law was remotely comparable to the depth and intensity of his Jewish experience. It would be like someone who had played a few games of pick-up basketball as a kid suggesting they played basketball like an NBA star!

Likewise, our "under the Law" experience is not in the same class as that of Paul and other devout Jews. We may have experienced a few of the same basics, but their involvement in the Law of Moses was drastically more intense and in-depth than ours was. Our experience of being "under the Law" is just a bit beyond what Paul described when he said,

> *Even Gentiles, who do not have God's written law, show that they know his law when they instinctively obey it, even without having heard it. They demonstrate that God's law is written in their hearts, for their own conscience and thoughts either accuse them or tell them they are doing right.*
>
> Romans 2:14-15 NLT

Countless individuals have testified of having a nominal church background before they understood the gospel and realized they needed to be born again. Some had a little knowledge of the Ten Commandments, added a few traditional, religious regulations, and that became their law.

Romans 2:14 KJV reads, "These, having not the law, are a law unto themselves." In other words, we essentially created our own version of the Law, and of course, we couldn't keep that. So we all—Jews and Gentiles—need the grace of the Lord Jesus Christ for our salvation.

In discussing the differences and similarities between the spiritual backgrounds of Jews and Gentiles, Paul said,

> *Should we conclude that we Jews are better than others? No, not at all, for we have already shown that all people, whether Jews or Gentiles, are under the power of sin.*
>
> *We are made right with God by placing our faith in Jesus Christ. And this is true for everyone who believes, no matter who we are.*
>
> *For everyone has sinned; we all fall short of God's glorious standard. Yet God, with undeserved kindness, declares that we are righteous. He did this through Christ Jesus when he freed us from the penalty for our sins.*
>
> Romans 3:9,22-24 NLT

Verse 24 in the New King James Version reads, "Being justified freely by His grace through the redemption that is in Christ Jesus." Regardless of our background, the issue of our salvation ultimately comes back to God's grace, not our performance.

Law Versus Grace

While attending our first year of Bible School (1979-80), Lisa and I felt impressed to travel to and preach in Australia. We established a connection with Peter Allard, who pastored a church and ran a Bible School in Wagga Wagga, New South Wales. Peter graciously hosted us that summer for seven weeks, set up an itinerary for us, and provided us with transportation.

While there, we came across a chart Peter had developed contrasting the Law and grace. It impacted me powerfully then and continues to bless me today, so I have adapted much of that material in the following. I believe it will bless you as well.

Old Testament Law	New Testament Grace
Imposes divine standards based on God's holiness for the purpose of revealing human sinfulness and making us aware of our need for divine assistance.	Imparts divine life based on God's benevolence for the purpose of making us a partaker of the divine nature and allowing us to fully partake of divine assistance.
The Law was given by Moses (John 1:17).	Grace and truth came by Jesus Christ (John 1:17).
Prohibits us from coming to God (Exodus 19:10-25; Hebrews 12:18-21).	Bids us to come as we are (John 6:37; Matthew 11:28-30).
Condemns the sinner (Romans 7:9-11).	Redeems the sinner (1 Peter 1:18-19; Ephesians 1:7).
Can never take away sin.	Purges the conscience by the blood of Christ (Hebrews 9:14).
Shuts every mouth (Romans 3:19).	Opens our mouths in praise to God.
Says, "Do this or die."	Says, "It is done, now live."
Says, "Try, do your best."	Says, "Trust, rest."
Condemns the best (Romans 3:20).	Justifies the worst (Romans 3:24).
Says, "Pay what you owe."	Says, "It is paid in full" (Romans 4:5; John 19:30).
Produces despair over our performance.	Produces rejoicing over Christ's performance.

Old Testament Law	New Testament Grace
Provides for the imputation of sin (Romans 4:15).	Provides for the impartation of righteousness.
Says, "The wages of sin is death" (Romans 6:23).	Says, "The gift of God is eternal life."
Says, "Give man the punishment he deserves."	Says, "Give man mercy that he has not deserved."
Says, "The soul that sins shall die" (Ezekiel 18:4).	Says, "Believe only and live" (Romans 4:3).
Reveals the sin of mankind (Romans 7:7).	Reveals God's love for mankind (Romans 5:6-8).
Grants us the knowledge of sin (Romans 3:20).	Grants us the knowledge of redemption (Ephesians 3:1-12).
Requires obedience (thou shalt not).	Gives us the power to obey (Ezekiel 36:27).
Demands that you meet requirements.	Invites you to receive blessings.
Written on stone (Exodus 32:15-16).	Written on the heart (2 Corinthians 3:3; Hebrews 10:16-17).
Had a certain glory (2 Corinthians 3:7-11).	Has a glory that supersedes and excels.
Its reign ended with Christ (Romans 10:4; 2 Corinthians 3:7).	Its reign endures (2 Corinthians 3:11).
Leaves a veil on the mind (2 Corinthians 3:12-16).	Unveils Christ to our hearts.
Brings us into bondage (Romans 7:1-2).	Sets us at liberty (2 Corinthians 3:17).

Old Testament Law	New Testament Grace
Reminds us of our sin.	Reminds us of Christ's finished work.
Something that we have to keep.	Something that keeps us.
Makes us sin-conscious.	Makes us Son-conscious.
Reveals and reinforces our separation from God.	Reveals and reinforces our union with God.
Deals in shadows (Colossians 2:17).	Deals in substance.
Ministers death to non-conformists.	Ministers life that conforms us to the image of Christ (Romans 8:29).
Focuses on sin in our lives.	Focuses on Christ in our lives.
Causes fear and despair.	Inspires faith and hope.
The Old Testament ends with a curse (Malachi 4:6).	The New Testament ends with a blessing (Rev. 22:21).

The law of Moses was unable to save us because of the weakness of our sinful nature. So God did what the law could not do. He sent his own Son in a body like the bodies we sinners have. And in that body God declared an end to sin's control over us by giving his Son as a sacrifice for our sins.

Romans 8:4 NLT

Chapter 12

SAVED TO WHAT?

As important as it is to know what God's grace has saved us from, it is equally vital to know what God's grace has saved us to. Grace is more than a parachute that saved us from a catastrophic fall; grace is a catalyst to propel us into a fruitful and productive life. This brings us to the topic of an often misunderstood issue: works.

In order to have a scriptural understanding of works as it relates to the grace of God, we must first realize that the New Testament speaks of many different types of works.

- Jesus decried the evil works of the world in John 7:7, the works of Cain are called evil in 1 John 3:12, and in 1 John 3:8 we read that Jesus came "to destroy the works of the devil."

- Paul repeatedly warned against works as a means of obtaining salvation in Romans 3:27; 4:2,4,6; 9:32; 11:6.

- Paul told believers to cast off the "works of darkness" (Romans 13:12) and expose them (Ephesians 5:11).

- In Colossians 1:21 Paul also speaks of "wicked works."

- In Galatians 5:19-21 we are warned not to indulge in the "works of the flesh," which include, "adultery, fornication, uncleanness, lewdness, idolatry, sorcery, hatred, contentions, jealousies, outbursts of wrath, selfish ambitions, dissensions, heresies, envy, murders, drunkenness, revelries, and the like."

- Hebrews 6:1 speaks of "repentance from dead works" as one of the foundational doctrines of Christ.

- Jesus said men would be rewarded, "each according to his works" (Matthew 16:27).

- Jesus often spoke of the works He did; see John 5:36; 9:4; 10:25, 32, 37-38; and 14:10-12.

- Jesus said the good works of His disciples would be a shining light, causing men to glorify God in Heaven (Matthew 5:16).

- Paul said good works should mark the life of a believer in Ephesians 2:10, 1 Timothy 2:10; 5:10, 25; 6:18; and 1 Peter 2:12.

- Speaking to the seven churches of Asia Minor, Jesus told every congregation, "I know your works" (Revelation 2:2, 9, 13, 19; 3:1, 8, 15), and then commended or reproved them.

The Root and the Fruit

When God's grace comes into our lives at the root level of salvation, His grace comes apart from our works. We don't do anything! We are not made new by God's grace plus our trying real hard, going to church regularly, or any work on our part. We simply receive His grace by faith.

> *God saved you by his grace when you believed. And you can't take credit for this; it is a gift from God. Salvation is not a reward for the good things we have done, so none of us can boast about it.*
>
> Ephesians 2:8-9 NLT

In this passage, Paul deals exclusively with grace as the root of our salvation. But if we only understand the root side of things, we might stop right there and say, "That's right. Our works have nothing to do with our salvation, so works are unimportant and irrelevant." That may be true concerning the root, but not the fruit. Jesus said His true followers would be known for their fruit (John 15:2,4-5,8,16).

> *For we are His workmanship, created in Christ Jesus for good works, which God prepared beforehand that we should walk in them.*
>
> Ephesians 2:10

The New Living Translation renders this verse, "For we are God's masterpiece. He has created us anew in Christ Jesus, so we can do the good things he planned for us long ago." God's grace does not save us based upon our works, but His grace inspires, enhances, invigorates, and energizes our works after we are saved. Our works express our salvation. We are to resist all temptations to do evil, wicked, legalistic, dead, dark, devilish, carnal, or fleshly works; but we are to obey the Word and the Spirit and be "fruitful in every good work" (Colossians 1:10).

Paul's Word to Titus

> *For we ourselves were also once foolish, disobedient, deceived, serving various lusts and pleasures, living in malice and envy, hateful and hating one another. But when the kindness and the love of God our Savior toward man appeared, not by works of righteousness which we have done, but according to His mercy He saved us, through the washing of regeneration and renewing of the Holy Spirit, whom He poured out on us abundantly through Jesus Christ our Savior, that having been justified by His grace we should become heirs according to the hope of eternal life.*
>
> Titus 3:3-7

Paul tells Titus what is repeated and emphasized frequently: Salvation is not by our works but by God's grace. The passage above declares the root of grace; the very next verse reveals the fruit of grace.

This is a faithful saying, and these things I want you to affirm constantly, that those who have believed in God should be careful to maintain good works. These things are good and profitable to men.

Titus 3:8

When it comes to producing salvation, the Bible says "no" to any work on our part. When it comes to expressing our salvation, the Bible says "yes" to our good works generated by God's grace. Are works the root of our salvation? Absolutely not. But are works the intended fruit of our salvation? Most certainly. Paul says, "Look Titus, you are saved by God's grace not by your works; but once you are saved, the grace of God inside of you is going to inspire you and empower you to do the works God calls you to do."

In all things showing yourself to be a pattern of good works.

Titus 2:7

...Jesus Christ, who gave Himself for us, that He might redeem us from every lawless deed and purify for Himself His own special people, zealous for good works.

Titus 2:13-14

And let our people also learn to maintain good works, to meet urgent needs, that they may not be unfruitful.

Titus 3:14

Was Paul, the man who said more about grace than anyone else, trying to put the believers under some kind of legalistic bondage by telling them they should work? Of course not. Paul understood that while grace imparts the gift of eternal life to believers apart from their works, grace is not some kind of doorway into spiritual irresponsibility and laziness.

Rather, grace is a springboard into a life of obedience and fruitfulness. Grace (divine empowerment in our lives) provides the impetus and is the very basis for our obedience to God, to do the works pleasing to Him and beneficial to others. **We are not saved by works, but we are saved to good works.**

Before we were born again, God's grace came to us and said, "It doesn't matter how many evil works you have done or how many good works you have done. You cannot have been so bad that you are beyond the reach of My mercy, and you cannot have been so good that you do not need My mercy. Regardless of how good or bad your life has been, I am here to impart My grace and forgiveness to you. I do this so you will have a brand new life filled with the good works I have ordained for you."

Having accepted His free gift, God's grace again (in essence) says to us, "Now that you are forgiven, accepted, and saved, I'm going to work in you and empower you to fulfill God's plan for your life."

Did James Contradict Paul?

Over the years many have sensed a tension between the apostles Paul and James in their writings. Some have contended they contradicted each other. Let's look at the verses people have mistakenly believed are in opposition to each other:

> *Knowing that a man is not justified by the works of the law but by faith in Jesus Christ, even we have believed in Christ Jesus, that we might be justified by faith in Christ and not by the works of the law; for by the works of the law no flesh shall be justified.*
>
> Galatians 2:16

> *You see then that a man is justified by works, and not by faith only.*
>
> James 2:24

A superficial reading of these two statements gives the impression of a contradiction, but a closer look reveals that Paul and James were addressing salvation from two different perspectives. Paul spoke of the root, while James was addressing the fruit.

Paul	James
Addressed those who had known freedom in Christ but were returning to Mosaic legalism.	Addressed those who gave mental assent to Christianity but had no fruit as evidence of their faith.
"Works of the Law" meant a legalistic compliance to Mosaic requirements.	"Works" meant corresponding actions that proceeded from true faith.
Addressed Mosaic works as a cause of salvation, and he said no.	Addressed good works as a result of salvation, and he said yes.
Defended true faith as opposed to the idea that we are saved by Jesus plus some work such as circumcision.	Defended true faith from dead orthodoxy (barren mental assent), which produced no fruit or evidence in the lives of believers.
Wanted believers to quit trusting in dead works and trust in Jesus alone for salvation.	Wanted believers to embrace good works as an expression of their faith in Jesus.

James was not rejecting faith as the basis of salvation; rather, he was promoting the idea that true saving faith is not dead, lifeless, and unproductive. He taught that faith was more than mere mental agreement, that genuine faith is inseparable from the actions it produces.

I can already hear one of you agreeing by saying, "Sounds good. You take care of the faith department, I'll handle the works department."

Not so fast. You can no more show me your works apart from your faith than I can show you my faith apart from my works. Faith and works, works and faith, fit together hand in glove.

Do I hear you professing to believe in the one and only God, but then observe you complacently sitting back as if you had done something wonderful? That's just great. Demons do that, but what good does it do them? Use your heads! Do you suppose for a minute that you can cut faith and works in two and not end up with a corpse on your hands?

Wasn't our ancestor Abraham "made right with God by works" when he placed his son Isaac on the sacrificial altar? Isn't it obvious that faith and works are yoked partners, that faith expresses itself in works? That the works are "works of faith"? The full meaning of "believe" in the Scripture sentence, "Abraham believed God and was set right with God," includes his action. It's that mesh of believing and acting that got Abraham named "God's friend." Is it not evident that a person is made right with God not by a barren faith but by faith fruitful in works?

The same with Rahab, the Jericho harlot. Wasn't her action in hiding God's spies and helping them escape—that seamless unity of believing and doing—what counted with God? The very moment you separate body and spirit, you end up with a corpse. Separate faith and works and you get the same thing: a corpse.

James 2:18-26 MSG

Paul Covered Both Bases

Let us go on and get past the elementary stage in the teachings and doctrine of Christ (the Messiah), advancing steadily toward the completeness and perfection that belong to spiritual maturity. Let us not again be laying the foundation of repentance and abandonment of dead works (dead formalism) and of the faith [by which you turned] to God.

Hebrews 6:1 AMP

Paul said that part of our elementary spiritual foundation involves repenting from and abandoning dead works (dead formalism or dead ritualism). These are the same types of "works of the Law" he denounced in the book of Galatians. Just a few chapters later, however, he promotes good works. Paul said, "And let us consider one another in order to stir up love and good works" (Hebrews 10:24). Both Paul and James were advocates of the right kind of works, those directed by God's will and inspired and empowered by His grace. We clearly see there are some types of works we are to reject and one type of work we are to walk in.

As we tap into and live from the grace of God within, may we be ever mindful that while our works do not produce salvation, they do express and are a witness to our new life in Jesus Christ. His phenomenal grace enables us to fulfill Jesus' commands with joy and gratitude in our hearts.

Let your light so shine before men, that they may see your good works and glorify your Father in heaven.

Matthew 5:16

Questions for Reflection and Discussion:

- What was new and fresh about saving grace to you?

- What reinforced the understanding you already had of saving grace?

- What challenged your previous or current understanding of saving grace?

- In what way does Mrs. Wilson's actions (in the *Dennis the Menace* illustration) reflect the nature and the actions of God toward you? Toward humanity?

- Many people (even in churches) still think if they are good enough, do enough good works, or lead a good enough life, they will make it to heaven. How prevalent was this type of thinking in your religious background? How did your perspective change from "try" to "trust?"

- Why didn't God just overlook or ignore sin?

- What would you share with a person who believed they could be righteous by keeping the Law or by being a good person?

- What does Paul's statement in 2 Corinthians 3:6, "For the letter kills, but the Spirit gives life" mean to you?

- What is meant by saying that the ceremonies of the Old Testament were merely shadows of good things yet to come?

- How can a person have a "law mentality" relative to God even if they were never Jewish?

- Describe the relationship between grace and works in terms of the root and the fruit.

- How did Paul and James present the idea of works relative to salvation? Did their views contradict or complement each other?

Part Four

Exactly How Does Grace Work in My Life?

Chapter 13

SANCTIFYING GRACE

But grow in the grace and knowledge of our Lord and Savior Jesus Christ.

2 Peter 3:18

G od's grace was instrumental in bringing us to God (saving grace), and now His grace is instrumental in our walk with God. God had grace for our initiation into His family, and He also has grace for our continuation with Him.

One aspect of God's grace that helps us in our ongoing walk with Him is what we call sanctifying grace.

- Sanctifying grace is God's power and ability purifying us and enabling us to live holy lives in a corrupt world.
- Sanctifying grace keeps us from being contaminated.
- Sanctifying grace is the impartation of God's holiness.
- Sanctifying grace is Love Cleansing.

And may the God of peace Himself sanctify you through and through [separate you from profane things, make you pure and wholly consecrated to God]; and may your spirit and soul and body be preserved sound and complete [and found] blameless at the coming of our Lord Jesus Christ (the Messiah).

1 Thessalonians 5:23 AMP

The word "sanctify" means "to make holy." In the Greek language, the words sanctify, saints, and holy are all related to one another. The word "saints" means "holy ones." Paul uses that word of all believers, meaning that they belong to God or are set apart unto God.

Two Sides of Truth

In order to truly appreciate sanctifying grace, it is important to understand both the legal and the experiential side of biblical truth. The following story helps us to understand these concepts.

Imagine a baby is born into a royal family and is the direct heir to the throne. From the moment that child is born, legally he is as much the heir to the throne as he will ever be, but experientially he is not exhibiting a lot of royal traits! He cries frequently (and loudly), soils his diapers, and spits up periodically. However, as he matures and develops, his parents train him to become—by demeanor and conduct—who he already is by inheritance.

Having put your faith in the Lord Jesus Christ, you are a child of God. If you were just born again yesterday and have not had time to mature, develop godly traits, or establish a track record of excellent Christian conduct, you are still God's child. You have a spiritual identity and inheritance that is yours by God's grace. As you grow and mature in your walk with the Lord, you also are becoming—by demeanor and conduct—who you are by inheritance.

Just as the child born to the king is heir to the throne and has many rights and privileges, every child of God can joyfully declare, "Because I am in Christ Jesus, I am:

- A branch abiding in the Vine (John 15:5)

- Justified (Romans 5:1)

- Dead to sin (Romans 6:11)

- Alive to God (Romans 6:11)

- Free from condemnation (Romans 8:1)

- An heir of God and a joint-heir with Jesus Christ (Romans 8:17)

- More than a conqueror (Romans 8:37)

- Inseparable from the love of God (Romans 8:39)

- Joined to the Lord, one spirit with Him (1 Corinthians 6:17)

- The temple of the Holy Spirit (1 Corinthians 6:19)

- Bought with a price (1 Corinthians 6:20)

- A member of the body of Christ (1 Corinthians 12:27)

- Always triumphant in Christ (2 Corinthians 2:14)

- A new creation in Christ Jesus (2 Corinthians 5:17)

- Reconciled to God (2 Corinthians 5:18)

- The righteousness of God in Christ (2 Corinthians 5:21)

- Redeemed from the curse of the law (Galatians 3:13)

- A son of God (Galatians 3:26)

- Abraham's seed, and an heir according to the promise (Galatians 3:29)

- Free (Galatians 5:1)

- A saint (Ephesians 1:1)

- Blessed with every spiritual blessing (Ephesians 1:3)

- Chosen (Ephesians 1:4)

- Accepted in the Beloved (Ephesians 1:6)

- Sealed with the Holy Spirit of promise (Ephesians 1:13)

- Seated with Christ in heavenly places (Ephesians 2:6)

- God's workmanship (Ephesians 2:10)

- A fellow citizen with the saints and a member of the household of God (Ephesians 2:19)

- A citizen of Heaven (Philippians 3:20)

- Delivered from the power of darkness and translated into the kingdom of God's dear Son (Colossians 1:13)

- Forgiven (Colossians 1:14)

- Complete in Christ (Colossians 2:10)

- A living stone (1 Peter 2:5)

- A partaker of the divine nature (2 Peter 1:4)

As we joyfully and boldly proclaim these truths, we renew our minds to our new identity in Christ. We are not bragging on ourselves; we are giving God glory for the work He has performed in our lives by His grace! As these truths become established in our hearts and reinforced in our minds, they enable us to resist the temptations and pressures of the world.

Having the right sense of identity helps you to make the right decisions, and eventually who you are legally is expressed richly in your lifestyle. However, you have an enemy who wants to hinder the sanctifying grace of God in your life. Satan is the accuser of the brethren (Revelation 12:10), and he does not want you to discover who you are in Christ. If he can keep you believing that your identity is defined by your past sins and failures, he can continue to dominate and oppress you. But when you discover who God's Word says you are and walk in the light of His Word, you will begin to reign as the royalty you were born to be.

Another enemy you can defeat through God's sanctifying grace is the negative thought patterns and old habits that tag along in your flesh after you have been born again. Peter advises how to deal with such things:

> So get rid of all evil behavior. Be done with all deceit, hypocrisy, jealousy, and all unkind speech. Like newborn babies, you must crave pure spiritual milk so that you will grow into a full experience of salvation. Cry out for this nourishment, now that you have had a taste of the Lord's kindness.
>
> 1 Peter 2:1-3 NLT

Think again about the baby born as heir to the throne. That baby is complete. He has ten fingers and ten toes. He has eyes, ears, a nose, and a mouth, but he has yet to grow into maturity and adulthood. Likewise, a child of God is complete in Christ (Colossians 2:10), but there is always a need for more maturity and understanding. Paul communicated this when he addressed the Corinthians. Legally, he said they were "sanctified in Christ Jesus" and "called to be saints" (1 Corinthians 1:2), "enriched in everything by Him" (1 Corinthians 1:5), and that they were "in Christ Jesus, who became for us wisdom from God—and righteousness and sanctification and redemption" (1 Corinthians 1:30). "In Christ" they sounded pretty good, didn't they? That's who they were and what they had. However, these legal realities did not hide the fact that there were attitudes and behaviors in their lives that needed to be radically transformed.

In 1 Corinthians 3:1,3 Paul called these same believers "babes in Christ" and said, "You are still carnal. For where there are envy, strife, and divisions among you, are you not carnal and behaving like mere men?" He also said that some of them were "puffed up" (1 Corinthians 4:18), or filled with pride.

There are two sides of a coin, and there are two sides to your life in Christ. There is your identity, or who you are in Christ, and there is your lifestyle; there is your position and your practice. Sanctifying grace brings the truth of your position in Christ into your outward conduct.

The New Testament addresses both your position and behavior.

Positional Truth	Behavioral Application
The legal side of who you are in Christ.	The experiential side that is evidenced by your walk in the world.
The root of who you are by God's grace.	The fruit of your life as you allow God's sanctifying grace to work in you.
Gifted into you.	Manifested through you.
Instantaneously imputed to you when you become a child of God.	Progressively expressed through you as you grow in, yield to, and obey God.
An event.	A process.
Declared to be so.	Seen to be so.
Based on Christ dwelling in you.	Based on Christ showing through you.
The Doctrine: This is what God's grace has done in and for you.	The Application: God's sanctifying grace empowers you to obey God's Word and His Spirit.

Grace is first and foremost about what God has done, but grace is also about what God enables you to do. What you do is based on what He has done. Paul communicated "the done and the do" repeatedly in his writings. For example, the first three chapters of Ephesians are predominantly positional truth, what God has done:

- We are blessed with every spiritual blessing in heavenly places.

- He chose us in Him before the foundation of the world.

- He made us accepted in the Beloved.

- In Him, we have redemption through His blood.

- In Him, we have obtained an inheritance.

- We have been made to sit in heavenly places in Christ Jesus.

- We were sealed with the Holy Spirit of promise.

In the next three chapters (Ephesians 4-6), we read about our response, how we are to live in our practice, or "the do":

- Walk worthy of our calling.

- Maintain unity amongst ourselves.

- Quit lying.

- Quit stealing.

- Be kind to each other, tenderhearted, forgiving one another.

- Walk in love.

- Let no fornication, uncleanness, or covetous be named among us.

- Be properly related to one another in our families and our work.

In his introduction to the book of Ephesians in *The Message*, Eugene Peterson eloquently writes,

What we know about God and what we do for God have a way of being broken apart in our lives. The moment the organic unity of belief and behavior is damaged in any way, we are incapable of living out the full humanity for which we were created. Paul's letter to the Ephesians joins together what has been torn apart in our sin-wrecked world. He begins with an exuberant exploration of what Christians believe about God, and then, like a surgeon skillfully setting a compound fracture, "sets" this belief in God into our behavior before God so that the bones—belief and behavior—knit together and heal.

Paul was a responsible minister of the truth. He taught both sides of the coin: First he laid the foundation of who we are and what we have in Christ, and then he described what that should look like to the people around us. Paul covered both sides of the issue: identity and practice, position and application, or as Peterson described it, belief and behavior.

Human Reasoning Versus Bible Truth

Some think that once we enter into a relationship with God, He only sees us as perfect in Christ. While it is true that God sees us through the eyes of redemption, He does not become oblivious to or disinterested in our conduct. Otherwise, the Holy Spirit would never have inspired the many New Testament passages that deal with corrections and adjustments that need to made in believers' lives.

Instead of adhering to the Word of God and embracing both sides of the issue, some have used faulty human reasoning to grossly distort God's grace. They encourage lines of thought like these:

- Since God's grace was not based upon our performance or perfection, God must not care how we live.

- Since God's love and acceptance is not based on our works, we are free to do whatever we want and live however we like.

- Since God only sees us in Christ, our behavior is of no consequence.

- Since God has already forgiven us of everything, sin doesn't matter.

Some have even adopted carnal and worldly lifestyles and proceed to defend such loose behavior by claiming to be "under grace," and they think this is totally acceptable to God.

Called the Apostle of Grace, Paul was aware that such reasoning could be misapplied to his teaching, and he went to great lengths to see that such distortions were addressed and corrected. For example, take Romans 5:20-21, where he emphasizes that God's grace is greater than our sin.

> *God's law was given so that all people could see how sinful they were. But as people sinned more and more, God's wonderful grace became more abundant. So just as sin ruled over all people and brought them to death, now God's wonderful grace rules instead, giving us right standing with God and resulting in eternal life through Jesus Christ our Lord.*
>
> Romans 5:20-21 NLT

This is a beautiful truth! But Paul knew how some people think. There are always a few who look for loopholes, so they can do what they want to do without feeling guilty or fearing negative consequences. All they read was, "But as people sinned more and more, God's wonderful grace became more abundant." Therefore they concluded, "If more sin results in more grace, we should sin more! Then we will get more of God's grace." In the next two verses, Paul slams the lid shut on that kind of errant thinking.

> *Well then, should we keep on sinning so that God can show us more and more of his wonderful grace? Of course not! Since we have died to sin, how can we continue to live in it?*
>
> Romans 6:1-2 NLT

If you are in Christ by God's saving grace, your reasonable response is to live according to His sanctifying grace, to think, speak, and act like Him.

Paul took his responsibility as a minister very seriously, and so he defended the truth of grace from both possible errors: legalism, or living by the Law; and lasciviousness, which is living by carnal desires. Paul was emphatic in defending his teaching from misrepresentations of his teaching:

> *Some people even slander us by claiming that we say, "The more we sin, the better it is!" Those who say such things deserve to be condemned.*
>
> Romans 3:8 NLT

Apparently, misunderstandings and distortions of Paul's teaching regarding grace were widespread. Even the apostle Peter felt a need to address the issue.

> *And so, dear friends, while you are waiting for these things to happen,* **make every effort to be found living peaceful lives that are pure and blameless in his sight.**
>
> *And remember, the Lord's patience gives people time to be saved. This is what our beloved brother Paul also wrote to you with the wisdom God gave him—speaking of these things in all of his letters. Some of his comments are hard to understand, and* **those who are ignorant and unstable have twisted his letters to mean something quite different,** *just as they do with other parts of Scripture. And this will result in their destruction.*
>
> *I am warning you ahead of time, dear friends.* **Be on guard so that you will not be carried away by the errors of these wicked people and lose your own secure footing. Rather, you must grow in the grace and knowledge of our Lord and Savior Jesus Christ.**
>
> *All glory to him, both now and forever! Amen.*
>
> 2 Peter 3:14-18 NLT (emphasis mine)

Peter was aware that some ignorant and unstable people were twisting Paul's teaching to their own destruction. He said these people were wicked, and associating with them could cause us to lose our secure footing. I believe Peter addressed this error because he said to, "make every effort to be found living peaceful lives that are pure and blameless in his sight" and told us to "grow in the grace and knowledge of our Lord and Savior Jesus Christ."

It is not accidental that Peter brought up these two issues in the immediate context of mentioning people who were distorting Paul's teachings. Both of these issues are vitally connected, but how? Growing in the true grace and knowledge of the Lord Jesus will lead us into living peaceful lives that are pure and blameless in God's sight. True grace and knowledge never lead us into sloppy, careless, impure, or sinful living. I believe the "twisting" Peter referred to involved individuals saying that grace means we can live however we want to, and that sinful behavior doesn't matter.

Grace is free and is not based upon our works. However, God's grace is not a hammock that lulls us into a sense of careless self-indulgence or moral insensitivity. Rather, God's grace is a launching pad that propels us into a life of obedience to God's Word and Spirit, spiritual growth, separation from evil, and dynamic discipleship.

Grace Trains Us

"He called them that they might be holy, and holiness is the beauty produced by His workmanship in them."

—Thomas Watson[1]

Paul wrote the following to Titus, a pastor under his guidance and supervision:

For the grace of God that brings salvation has appeared to all men, teaching us that, denying ungodliness and worldly lusts, we should live

soberly, righteously, and godly in the present age, looking for the blessed
hope and glorious appearing of our great God and Savior Jesus Christ,
who gave Himself for us, that He might redeem us from every lawless
deed and purify for Himself His own special people, zealous for good
works.

Titus 2:11-14

Isn't that rich? God's grace teaches us. The word "teaching" means "to train (as in parents training children), to instruct, to chastise, and to correct."[2] Consider the way two other translations render verse 12:

It teaches us to say "No" to ungodliness and worldly passions, and to live
self-controlled, upright and godly lives in this present age.

NIV

We're being shown how to turn our backs on a godless, indulgent life,
and how to take on a God-filled, God-honoring life. This new life is
starting right now.

MSG

Grace is never divine permission to do wrong. Grace is divine empowerment to do what is right.

A pastor was troubled when he shared a story with me. He said that a couple had visited his church, and he noticed they had different last names but the same address. After they had attended a few times, he was able to visit with them personally. They unashamedly told him they were not married and were living together. Pastors realize that some people are not born again and don't know what the Bible says about such things, but to the pastor's surprise this couple had been saved and involved in churches for many years.

They proceeded to tell him that since they had received this new revelation of God's grace, they had come to realize they were free to live together because Jesus had already died for all sins: past, present, and future. Shocked by their theology, he proceeded to tell them the biblical truth their "new revelation" had conveniently omitted.

God's grace must never be isolated from the rest of the teaching of the New Testament. Scriptural grace is always integrated and works seamlessly with everything else God tells us in the Bible. Actually, God's grace enables us to carry out every assignment He asks of us, whether it comes from the Word or the Spirit. We are to live by "every word that proceeds from the mouth of God" (Matthew 4:4). Unfortunately, this couple was taking one aspect of grace, saving grace, while completely disregarding sanctifying grace.

Grace is in no way a license to sin. I'm not saying we become flawlessly perfect or that we will never need God's forgiveness again. James said, "For we all stumble in many things" (James 3:2). But born again children of God who are growing in grace, growing in the Word, and are being led by God's Spirit are not looking to use grace as an excuse, a pretext, or a cop-out for engaging in sinful, self-indulgent behavior. Grace trains and empowers us to say no to sin and to rise above the carnality that is so prevalent in this world.

God's sanctifying grace is not passively against sin. It does not train us by saying, "It's probably a good idea not to sin, but it's okay if you do." Sanctifying grace is actively and vehemently against sin. It says, "I'm going to lead you and show you how to cooperate with My influence so that you live free from the power of sin."

Jude Weighs In

Jude, like Paul and Peter, was also aware of distortions and perversions to the message of God's grace. Though his only epistle in the New Testament is comprised of one fairly brief chapter, it does not lack in power or conviction. Jude said:

Beloved, while I was very diligent to write to you concerning our common salvation, I found it necessary to write to you exhorting you to contend earnestly for the faith which was once for all delivered to the saints. For certain men have crept in unnoticed, who long ago were marked out for this condemnation, **ungodly men, who turn the grace of our God into lewdness** *and deny the only Lord God and our Lord Jesus Christ.*

Jude 3-4 (bold mine)

The word "lewdness" covers the gamut of an entire lack of moral restraint. Jude condemned those who taught that God's grace freed believers to do whatever they wanted to do. Their doctrine was two-fold: First, if it feels good, do it. Second, whatever you do is okay and will have no consequences because God's grace has everything covered.

Other translations shed additional light on verse 4.

- NLT: "Some ungodly people have wormed their way into your churches, saying that God's marvelous grace allows us to live immoral lives."

- RSV: "…ungodly persons who pervert the grace of our God into licentiousness."

- NIV[11]: "…ungodly people, who pervert the grace of our God into a license for immorality."

- NCV: "They are against God and have changed the grace of God into a reason for sexual sin."

God's grace—His sanctifying grace—is not dismissive toward and does not make light of sin. Rather, His sanctifying grace trains us to walk free from the power and influence of sin.

Did Jesus Die for All Sins?

But this Man, after He had offered one sacrifice for sins forever, sat down at the right hand of God.

Hebrews 10:12

In a legal sense, Jesus did die for all sins: past, present, and future. If He hadn't, every time someone sinned He would have to go back to the Cross and die again. However, this does not mean that we are free to sin flippantly, blatantly disregarding the overwhelming consensus of New Testament Scripture that clearly directs us to live holy lives, set good examples, and be conformed to the image of Jesus Christ by submitting to the training of grace.

Some who have embraced a twisted version of grace, believing it allows them to live however they desire, are quick to cry, "Legalism!" if anyone mentions scriptures that pertain to holiness, obedience, and living godly lives. As Leonard Ravenhill once said, "When there's something in the Bible that churches don't like, they call it 'legalism.'" These same individuals will often protest any kind of biblical directive, saying such things as:

- "I'm not under the Law."

- "You're not going to put me in bondage."

- "I've been set free from a religion of do's and don'ts."

God's grace is not a cop-out for believers to evade the responsibility of obeying the comprehensive teachings of the New Testament. Actually, God's grace leads us into obedience, not away from it. Again, I like to think of the word *responsibility* as our response to His ability. Certainly God has forgiveness for us if and when we miss it, but God's grace can supply the ability to help us get it right, not just the mercy to be forgiven when we get it wrong (1 John 2:1).

Whatever God has commanded us to do (and there are many directives in the New Testament for believers which have nothing to do with legalism), He will also give us the ability to obey. The ability that God gives us to carry out His commandments is His grace. When it comes to developing a lifestyle and behavior that is pleasing to God, His sanctifying grace is present to empower us.

Work hard to show the results of your salvation, obeying God with deep reverence and fear. For God is working in you, giving you the desire and the power to do what pleases him.

Philippians 2:12-13 NLT

I especially like how the Amplified Bible renders this passage.

Work out (cultivate, carry out to the goal, and fully complete) your own salvation with reverence and awe and trembling (self-distrust, with serious caution, tenderness of conscience, watchfulness against temptation, timidly shrinking from whatever might offend God and discredit the name of Christ).

[Not in your own strength] for it is God Who is all the while effectually at work in you [energizing and creating in you the power and desire], both to will and to work for His good pleasure and satisfaction and delight.

Thank God we don't have to do all of this in our natural ability! God imparts His supernatural power and might for the sanctification process, having made His grace—His divine ability—available to work in us and through us. I particularly like the part that says He helps us desire to do right. If we find it hard to be willing, we can ask Him to help us become willing!

In the *New King James Version*, Philippians 2:12 is very much to the point: "Work out your own salvation with fear and trembling." Notice Paul did not say "Work for your salvation." Rather, he said, "Work out your salvation." He is not talking about earning our salvation; he's talking about expressing our salvation.

What will sanctifying grace produce in our lives?

- Power to carry out the will of God.

- Power to be conformed to the image of Christ Jesus.

- Power to defeat carnality, sin, and worldly corruption.

- A godly lifestyle which is a powerful witness to the Lordship of Jesus Christ.

Jesus prayed in John 17:17, "Sanctify them by Your truth. Your word is truth." If Jesus prayed for us to be sanctified, do you think you can be sanctified? Do you think God will answer Jesus' prayer? As you read each of the following scriptures, say to yourself, "If God has asked me to do this, then I know His sanctifying grace will enable me do this."

I speak in human terms because of the weakness of your flesh. For just as you presented your members as slaves of uncleanness, and of lawlessness leading to more lawlessness, **so now present your members as slaves of righteousness for holiness.**

Romans 6:19 (bold mine)

I plead with you to **give your bodies to God** *because of all he has done for you. Let them be a living and holy sacrifice—the kind he will find acceptable. This is truly the way to worship him.* **Don't copy the behavior and customs of this world, but let God transform you into a new person by changing the way you think.**

Romans 12:1-2 NLT (bold mine)

Clothe yourself with the presence of the Lord Jesus Christ. And don't let yourself think about ways to indulge your evil desires.

Romans 13:14 NLT

Run from sexual sin! No other sin so clearly affects the body as this one does. For sexual immorality is a sin against your own body. **Don't you realize that your body is the temple of the Holy Spirit,** *who lives in you and was given to you by God? You do not belong to yourself, for God bought you with a high price. So* **you must honor God with your body.**

1 Corinthians 6:18-20 NLT (bold mine)

Therefore, having these promises, beloved, let us cleanse ourselves from all filthiness of the flesh and spirit, perfecting holiness in the fear of God.

2 Corinthians 7:1

The Fear of God

The remarkable thing about fearing God is that when you fear God you fear nothing else, whereas if you do not fear God, you fear everything else.

—Oswald Chambers[3]

In 2 Corinthians 7:1 above, Paul told the Corinthians they were to cleanse themselves from all filthiness and perfect holiness, and they were to do so "in the fear of God." I don't think this is referring to a natural fear, like being afraid of a rattlesnake or a tornado. Paul is talking about the reverence, awe, and respect we have for our Father's authority and power over the entire universe.

- "The fear of the LORD is clean, enduring forever" (Psalm 19:9).

- "The fear of the LORD is to hate evil" (Proverbs 8:13).

- "By the fear of the LORD one departs from evil" (Proverbs 16:6).

- "Then the churches throughout all Judea, Galilee, and Samaria had peace and were edified. And walking in the fear of the Lord and in the comfort of the Holy Spirit, they were multiplied" (Acts 9:31).

- "...submitting to one another in the fear of God" (Ephesians 5:21).

The fear of the Lord is not merely an Old Testament concept that is meaningless today. This phrase represents a principle that transcends all covenants, being used in both Old and New Testaments. While Solomon realized the fear of God caused people to hate and depart from evil when he wrote the book of Proverbs, Paul, the Apostle of Grace, wrote, "hate what is evil [loathe all ungodliness, turn in horror from wickedness], but hold fast to that which is good" (Romans 12:9 AMP).

Christians ask, "Which will help me live a holier life: the fear of God or the grace of God?" That is like asking, "Which wing is more important for this airplane to fly: the left wing or the right wing?" If we are going to fly successfully, we need both wings. If we are going to live successful Christian lives, we must walk in the fear of God and the grace of God. The right kind of fear (the reverential awe and respect for God) and the grace of God (that saves and makes all things possible—even overcoming sin) are not contradictory; they are complementary. John Newton addressed both kinds of fear in "Amazing Grace" when he wrote, "'Twas grace that taught my heart to fear, and grace my fears relieved."

More Admonitions from Paul

For you, brethren, have been called to liberty; only **do not use liberty as an opportunity for the flesh,** *but through love serve one another. I say then: Walk in the Spirit, and you shall not fulfill the lust of the flesh.*

Galatians 5:13,16 (bold mine)

In verse 16 Paul did not say, "Don't fulfill the lust of the flesh, and you will walk in the Spirit." No, the emphasis was on the positive. Focus on walking in the Spirit and you will not fulfill the lust of the flesh. Throw yourself into the positive power of God. Pursue obedience based on God's ability within you, tap into His spiritual DNA of sanctifying grace inside, and the lusts and temptations of your flesh will weaken and lose their ability to dominate you.

> *...that you* **put off, concerning your former conduct, the old man** *which grows corrupt according to the deceitful lusts, and be renewed in the spirit of your mind, and that you* **put on the new man** *which was created according to God, in true righteousness and holiness.*
>
> Ephesians 4:22-24 (bold mine)

> *Therefore* **put to death your members which are on the Earth:** *fornication, uncleanness, passion, evil desire, and covetousness, which is idolatry. Because of these things the wrath of God is coming upon the sons of disobedience, in which you yourselves once walked when you lived in them.*
>
> *But now* **you yourselves are to put off all these:** *anger, wrath, malice, blasphemy, filthy language out of your mouth.*
>
> Colossians 3:5-8 (bold mine)

> *Finally, dear brothers and sisters,* **we urge you in the name of the Lord Jesus to live in a way that pleases God,** *as we have taught you. You live this way already, and we encourage you to do so even more. For you remember what we taught you by the authority of the Lord Jesus.*
>
> **God's will is for you to be holy, so stay away from all sexual sin.** *Then each of you will control his own body and* **live in holiness and honor**—*not in lustful passion like the pagans who do not know God and his ways. Never harm or cheat a Christian brother in this matter by violating his wife, for the Lord avenges all such sins, as we have*

solemnly warned you before. **God has called us to live holy lives, not impure lives.** *Therefore, anyone who refuses to live by these rules is not disobeying human teaching but is rejecting God, who gives his Holy Spirit to you.*

1 Thessalonians 4:1-8 NLT (bold mine)

In a wealthy home some utensils are made of gold and silver, and some are made of wood and clay. The expensive utensils are used for special occasions, and the cheap ones are for everyday use. **If you keep yourself pure, you will be a special utensil for honorable use.** *Your life will be clean, and you will be ready for the Master to use you for every good work.*

Run from anything that stimulates youthful lusts. Instead, pursue righteous living, faithfulness, love, and peace. Enjoy the companionship of those who call on the Lord with pure hearts.

2 Timothy 2:20-22 NLT

- Present your members as slaves of righteousness for holiness.

- Give your bodies to God.

- Don't copy the behavior and customs of this world.

- Don't think about ways to indulge your evil desires.

- Run from sexual sin.

- Honor God with your body.

- Cleanse yourself from all filthiness of the flesh and spirit.

- Do not use liberty as an opportunity for the flesh.

- Walk in the Spirit and you shall not fulfill the lusts of the flesh.

- Live in a way that pleases God.

- Live holy, not ungodly lives.

Was Paul being legalistic in commanding us to live like this? Was he trying to get us to go back to keeping the Law in our own strength? Absolutely not! He was merely encouraging us to cooperate with the grace of God. If we walk in the Spirit, we will be supernaturally enabled to keep His Word.

Paul understood more than anyone that believers are new creatures in Christ and have received forgiveness and a new identity as children of God. This is positional truth, who we are in Him. But he also realized that we must "walk out" or "work out" this new identity in our behavior, conduct, and lifestyle. He also recognized we will never accomplish this in our own strength; we need the power of God's grace in our lives.

I don't believe Paul wants us to sit around thinking, "Okay, I've got to obey all these rules. I can't do this, and I can't do that." He was not instructing us to focus on "Thou shalt not," being "sin-conscious." He instructed us to be Jesus-conscious and focus on what He has told us to do. Reminds me of something I heard as a very young believer, that if we are busy doing the dos, we won't have time to do the don'ts.

We still deal with temptations, and Paul was not the only one who understood the role grace plays in our ability to lead an overcoming life. Peter opened his first epistle with the greeting, "Grace to you and peace be multiplied" (1 Peter 1:2). He did not advocate grace at the beginning of his letter and then proceed to pile a bunch of legalism upon his readers. He did, however, explain how God's sanctifying grace works in our lives to produce changed lives and lifestyles.

> *So you must live as God's obedient children. Don't slip back into your old ways of living to satisfy your own desires. You didn't know any better then. But now you must be holy in everything you do, just as God who chose you is holy. For the Scriptures say, "You must be holy because I am holy."*

> 1 Peter 1:14-16 NLT

Dear friends, I warn you as "temporary residents and foreigners" to keep away from worldly desires that wage war against your very souls.

It is God's will that your honorable lives should silence those ignorant people who make foolish accusations against you. For you are free, yet you are God's slaves, so **don't use your freedom as an excuse to do evil.**

1 Peter 2:11,15-16 NLT (bold mine)

You won't spend the rest of your lives chasing your own desires, but you will be anxious to do the will of God. You have had enough in the past of the evil things that godless people enjoy—their immorality and lust, their feasting and drunkenness and wild parties, and their terrible worship of idols.

Of course, your former friends are surprised when you no longer plunge into the flood of wild and destructive things they do. So they slander you.

1 Peter 4:2-4 NLT

As amazing as it sounds, some believers are accused—not just by unsaved people but by other Christians, especially compromising Christians—for being religious, under the Law, or holier-than-thou simply because they choose to live according to the principles of Scripture. They are ridiculed because they have allowed God's grace to do a sanctifying work in their lives and disciplined themselves to live holy lives.

Here are some simple guidelines concerning holiness:

Holiness is NOT	Holiness IS
External compliance to regulations made by people not God	Thinking, speaking, and acting like Jesus
Gritting your teeth and trying to conquer sin in your own power	Yielding to His sanctifying grace within and allowing Him to help you change
Posturing and pretending	Being and doing honestly
Looking down at others, thinking you are better than them	Being responsible for your own attitude and conduct
Thinking you are right and everyone else is wrong	Knowing God is right and humbly aligning yourself with Him
Endeavoring to measure up to a person's opinion of what is right	Allowing the Holy Spirit to transform your life
Achieved from the outside in	Expressed from the inside out

God's grace is not a cop-out or a cover-up for continuing in wrong behavior. His grace is the basis and the impetus behind transformed lives and godly lifestyles. Sanctifying grace speaks to the fact that God's very own power is at work within us, enabling us to be the people He has called us to be and to do the things He has commanded us to do. Sanctifying grace means we don't have to accomplish this apart from Him, but we find the power to obey and honor Him by virtue of cooperating with His power and grace at work within us.

Chapter 14

STRENGTHENING GRACE

We pray that you'll have the strength to stick it out over the long haul—not the grim strength of gritting your teeth but the glory-strength God gives. It is strength that endures the unendurable and spills over into joy, thanking the Father who makes us strong enough to take part in everything bright and beautiful that he has for us.

Colossians 1:11-12 MSG

L egendary football coach Vince Lombardi made a fascinating observation about what happens when people get worn out. He said, "Fatigue makes cowards of us all."[1] Vance Havner, a noted Baptist preacher, said, "Satan does some of his worst work on exhausted Christians, when nerves are frayed and the mind is faint."[2]

Just how big of an issue is being tired and fatigued in peoples' lives today? Consider all the commercials selling mattresses to help you get a better night's sleep, and the prevalence of coffee and energy drinks to help you get through the day. It would appear that we live in a society of tired people. If you ask a primary care physician, they will tell you that fatigue is a very common problem.

Because I am a Bible teacher and not a doctor or mattress salesman, I will approach this topic from the spiritual perspective of God's strengthening grace.

- Strengthening grace is God's power and ability to energize and inspire us to live victoriously, to reign over the challenges and circumstances of life.

- Strengthening grace keeps us from being defeated.

- Strengthening grace is the impartation of God's might.

- Strengthening grace is Love Empowering.

It should come as no surprise that God's grace is a source of strength to believers. Throughout the Old Testament, He freely gave strength to His people. The following verses have been loved, believed, and quoted for centuries, encouraging and comforting God's people in challenging times.

> *The LORD is my strength and song,*
> > *And He has become my salvation.*
>
> Exodus 15:2

> *The joy of the LORD is your strength.*
>
> Nehemiah 8:10

> *The LORD is the strength of my life;*
> > *Of whom shall I be afraid?*
> *Wait on the LORD;*
> > *Be of good courage,*
> > *And He shall strengthen your heart.*
>
> Psalm 27:1,14

> *The LORD will give strength to His people;*
> > *The LORD will bless His people with peace.*
>
> Psalm 29:11

But the salvation of the righteous is from the LORD;
    He is their strength in the time of trouble.

Psalm 37:39

God is our refuge and strength,
    A very present help in trouble.

Psalm 46:1

He gives power to the weak,
    And to those who have no might He increases strength.

Isaiah 40:29

A Constant Infusion

As we move into the New Testament, the Lord continues to impart strength to His people. He has an ever-present and abundant supply of His might for us. No doubt many believers, when faced with the drain and the weariness life brings, have personalized Philippians 4:13 and declared with the apostle Paul,

"I can do all things through Christ who strengthens me."

It is important to note that this verse does not say, "I can do all things through him who strengthen**ed** me," past tense, as though God had just given us one, limited dose of strength that has to last us for a lifetime. The verb *strengthens* denotes continuous action. That's a pretty amazing concept! Christ is infusing strength in Paul all the time, and I don't believe He is a respecter of persons. If He constantly infused Paul with strength, then He is constantly infusing strength in you and me.

For Paul, strength from God was not some kind of fringe benefit; it was an absolute necessity. The wear and tear that ministry had on him was horrific, something that most of us can only attempt to imagine. Some have had the idea that if a person has faith and is in the will of God, he will never face difficult times. If that was true, Paul had no faith and was seldom in the will of God.

Here is the context in which he made this statement:

I have learned how to be content (satisfied to the point where I am not disturbed or disquieted) in whatever state I am.

I know how to be abased and live humbly in straitened circumstances, and I know also how to enjoy plenty and live in abundance. I have learned in any and all circumstances the secret of facing every situation, whether well-fed or going hungry, having a sufficiency and enough to spare or going without and being in want.

I have strength for all things in Christ Who empowers me [I am ready for anything and equal to anything through Him Who infuses inner strength into me; I am self-sufficient in Christ's sufficiency].

Philippians 4:11-13 AMP

During his life and ministry, Paul faced the good, the bad, and the ugly. He learned that God was not just the God who reigned on sunny days when the birds were singing, but also during the storms and through the valleys of life. The following statements are even more revealing as to just how much Paul needed God's strengthening grace in his life.

I have worked harder, been put in prison more often, been whipped times without number, and faced death again and again. Five different times the Jewish leaders gave me thirty-nine lashes. Three times I was beaten with rods. Once I was stoned. Three times I was shipwrecked. Once I spent a whole night and a day adrift at sea. I have traveled on many long journeys. I have faced danger from rivers and from robbers. I have faced danger from my own people, the Jews, as well as from the Gentiles. I have faced danger in the cities, in the deserts, and on the seas. And I have faced danger from men who claim to be believers but are not. I have worked hard and long, enduring many sleepless nights.

I have been hungry and thirsty and have often gone without food. I have shivered in the cold, without enough clothing to keep me warm.

Then, besides all this, I have the daily burden of my concern for all the churches.

2 Corinthians 11:23-28 NLT

When we arrived in Macedonia, there was no rest for us. We faced conflict from every direction, with battles on the outside and fear on the inside.

2 Corinthians 7:5 NLT

The Bible clearly says that Paul went through times of feeling weak and tired, and yet he overcame them through God's strengthening grace. He says in 2 Corinthians 11:27 NKJV, "in weariness and toil, in sleeplessness often," and yet in Colossians 1:29 AMP he says, "For this I labor [unto weariness], striving with all the superhuman energy which He so mightily enkindles and works within me."

That last verse provides rich insight into Paul's incredible endurance and amazing accomplishments. How could someone face so much hatred and abuse, so many beatings and imprisonments, and so many horrible conditions and deprivations? Paul was not oblivious to the physical and emotional toll that such hardships took on him, but he was also keenly aware that he was not carrying out his ministry by the limitations of his own natural resources; he was "striving with all the superhuman energy which He so mightily enkindles and works within me." Paul had learned to receive the constant infusion of the strengthening grace of God.

The Learning Process

Receiving a constant infusion of strengthening grace does not appear to have been automatic in Paul's life. Leading up to his powerful declaration in Philippians 4:13 ("I can do all things through Christ who strengthens me"), he said, "I have learned in whatever state I am, to be content" (Philippians 4:11). This whole process was not instantaneous, and that should give us hope! The same God who was patient with Paul will also be patient with us as we learn to be content and receive a constant infusion of His strengthening grace.

There is probably no other place where Paul's learning process is more vividly displayed than his description of his encounters with what he termed "a thorn in the flesh." He said it was a "messenger of Satan" assigned to "buffet" him (2 Corinthians 12:7). Many theories exist concerning what this thorn was, but this statement is made right after Paul listed all the beatings, imprisonments, persecutions, and other trials he went through (2 Corinthians 11:23-27). Therefore, it seems reasonable that this thorn in the flesh was an evil spirit, who incited harassment, abuse, torment, and discouragement toward Paul at every opportunity. I believe this spirit worked through people and circumstances in an attempt to so demoralize him that he would quit preaching the gospel, particularly the gospel of grace. In light of this, consider Paul's prayer and the Lord's response in this matter:

> Concerning this thing I pleaded with the Lord three times that it might depart from me. And He said to me, "My grace is sufficient for you, for My strength is made perfect in weakness." Therefore most gladly I will rather boast in my infirmities, that the power of Christ may rest upon me. Therefore I take pleasure in infirmities, in reproaches, in needs, in persecutions, in distresses, for Christ's sake. For when I am weak, then I am strong.
>
> 2 Corinthians 12:8-10

I have heard some say that Paul prayed, but the Lord said no. I don't see that. Granted, He did not respond nor had He ever promised that Paul would be able to go through life trouble-free. But His response to Paul was in the affirmative. He said, "My grace is sufficient for you." What did Jesus mean by this? The thorn was Satan's power directed against Paul. Grace was God's power released toward Paul. The Lord was saying that His power working in Paul and on Paul's behalf was greater than the power of Satan that was arrayed against him.

Read this passage (2 Corinthians 12:9, bold mine) again and notice the correlation between grace, strength, and power.

> *"***My grace*** is sufficient for you, for* **My strength** *is made perfect in weakness." Therefore most gladly I will rather boast in my infirmities, that* **the power of Christ** *may rest upon me.*

The Lord speaks in the first part, and Paul speaks in the last part. They use these three terms interchangeably:

- My grace (the Lord's grace)
- My strength (the Lord's strength)
- The power of Christ

Remember, Paul went through a learning process. In verse 8 he wanted the problem to go away, but by verse 10 his entire perspective had changed. He said,

> *So for the sake of Christ, I am well pleased and take pleasure in infirmities, insults, hardships, persecutions, perplexities and distresses;* **for when I am weak [in human strength], then am I [truly] strong (able, powerful in divine strength).**
>
> 2 Corinthians 12:10 AMP (bold mine)

When we are proud, self-reliant, and self-sufficient, we do not yield to the strengthening grace of God. We walk in our natural ability instead the power of God's strengthening grace. Paul learned that these divine infusions of strength came when he recognized his need for such strength. James 4:6 says, "But He gives more grace. Therefore He says: 'God resists the proud, But gives grace to the humble.'" Did you catch that? More grace! God gives more grace when a person humbly acknowledges his need for such grace.

> *For we do not want you to be ignorant, brethren, of our trouble which came to us in Asia: that we were burdened beyond measure, above strength, so that we despaired even of life. Yes, we had the sentence of death in ourselves,* **that we should not trust in ourselves but in God who raises the dead,** *who delivered us from so great a death, and does deliver us; in whom we trust that He will still deliver us.*
>
> 2 Corinthians 1:8-10 (bold mine)

Having learned to tap into the strengthening grace of God, Paul was quick to pass on this truth to his spiritual son, Timothy. Right before he told Timothy to "endure hardship as a good soldier of Jesus Christ" (2 Timothy 2:3), he pointed Timothy to the true source of power and endurance, "Timothy, my dear son, be strong through the grace that God gives you in Christ Jesus" (2 Timothy 2:1 NLT).

Grace Is Not Just for Crises

There seems to be a natural tendency for people to think they only need God in times of crisis, yet the Bible makes it clear that God wants "in" on everything. He never intended for our relationship with Him to be dormant except when we face trouble. He desires for us to lean upon Him and trust Him at all times. Paul learned the most about strengthening grace when he was in a situation that exceeded his ability to endure, but I believe he also learned to lean on God's strengthening grace as a lifestyle.

> *I have been crucified with Christ [in Him I have shared His crucifixion]; it is no longer I who live, but Christ (the Messiah) lives in me;*

and the life I now live in the body I live by faith in (by adherence to and reliance on and complete trust in) the Son of God, Who loved me and gave Himself up for me.

Galatians 2:20 AMP

Not only is Christ's righteousness ours, but His strength is ours as well. What a glorious day when we cease fleshly strivings and become what only the power of God can make us to be! This means we have stopped looking to God as a mere supplement to our lives and have realized He is our life! Even in the Old Testament there was a sharp distinction made between those who trusted in flesh and those who trusted in God.

This is what the LORD says:
"Cursed are those who put their trust in mere humans,
   who rely on human strength
   and turn their hearts away from the LORD.
They are like stunted shrubs in the desert,
   with no hope for the future.
They will live in the barren wilderness,
   in an uninhabited salty land.
"But blessed are those who trust in the LORD
   and have made the LORD their hope and confidence.
They are like trees planted along a riverbank,
   with roots that reach deep into the water.
Such trees are not bothered by the heat
   or worried by long months of drought.
Their leaves stay green,
   and they never stop producing fruit."

Jeremiah 17:5-8 NLT

We should trust in the Lord and make Him our hope and confidence as a lifestyle. Jeremiah said we would bear fruit in all seasons, and that is just what Jesus indicated would happen in John 15:5, when He said, "I am the vine, you are the branches. He who abides in Me, and I in him, bears much fruit; for without Me you can do nothing."

The ideal lifestyle for a Christian is to abide in Jesus 24-7, to continually receive His infusion of strengthening grace and walk in an ongoing awareness of His presence and His work. Then, when a crisis does arise, we have no hindrance in receiving His strength for the situation.

> *Let us therefore come boldly to the throne of grace, that we may obtain mercy and find grace to help in time of need.*
>
> Hebrews 4:16

What a wonderful invitation and promise! We don't need to come apologetically or timidly. We can come to Him with confidence to obtain the grace, mercy, wisdom, and power our situation requires.

Stay Infused with Grace

Below are several other passages of Scripture that reveal grace at work in our lives, strengthening us and giving us encouragement. Notice how God's grace, when operative and received, produces tangible results.

> *And with great power the apostles gave witness to the resurrection of the Lord Jesus. And great grace was upon them all.*
>
> Acts 4:33

> *When he [Barnabas] came and had seen the grace of God, he was glad, and encouraged them all that with purpose of heart they should continue with the Lord.*
>
> Acts 11:23

So now, brethren, I commend you to God and to the word of His grace, which is able to build you up and give you an inheritance among all those who are sanctified.

Acts 20:32

Those who receive abundance of grace and of the gift of righteousness will reign in life through the one, Jesus Christ.

Romans 5:17

Let no corrupt word proceed out of your mouth, but what is good for necessary edification, that it may impart grace to the hearers.

Ephesians 4:29

Let your speech always be with grace, seasoned with salt, that you may know how you ought to answer each one.

Colossians 4:6

Let the word of Christ dwell in you richly in all wisdom, teaching and admonishing one another in psalms and hymns and spiritual songs, singing with grace in your hearts to the Lord.

Colossians 3:16

It is good that the heart be established by grace.

Hebrews 13:9

But may the God of all grace, who called us to His eternal glory by Christ Jesus, after you have suffered a while, perfect, establish, strengthen, and settle you. To Him be the glory and the dominion forever and ever. Amen.

By Silvanus, our faithful brother as I consider him, I have written to you briefly, exhorting and testifying that this is the true grace of God in which you stand.

1 Peter 5:10-12

Have the Right Identity

At one time you were lost and separated from God, but that is no longer true. You are God's beloved, His son or daughter, and heir to all His promises. Knowing this truth and living in this reality is essential to appropriating God's strengthening grace in every area of your life. Your focus should be on who you are in Christ, not on who you were without Him.

The New Testament epistles are full of wonderful insights as to who God's grace has made you to be. With humility and boldness, you can triumphantly proclaim: "I am who God says I am, I have what God says I have, and I can do what God says I can do." I encourage you to make these declarations out loud.

I am...

- A new creation (2 Corinthians 5:17)

- The righteousness of God in Christ (2 Corinthians 5:21)

- Accepted in the Beloved (Ephesians 1:6)

- A new man created in righteousness and true holiness (Ephesians 4:24)

- A child of God, an heir of God, a joint-heir with Jesus Christ (Romans 8:16-17)

- His workmanship, created in Christ Jesus (Ephesians 2:10)

- Delivered from the power of darkness and have been translated into the kingdom of God's dear Son (Colossians 1:13)

- Free from the law of sin and death (Romans 8:2)

- An overcomer, because greater is He that is in me, than he that is in the world (1 John 4:4)

- More than a conqueror through Him who loves me (Romans 8:37)

- Quickened with Christ, raised with Christ, and seated with Christ in heavenly places (Ephesians 2:6)

I have...

- The Word of God (2 Peter 1:4)

- The name of Jesus (John 16:23-24; Mark 16:17-18)

- The presence of God (Hebrews 13:5-6)

- The armor of God (Ephesians 6:13-17)

- The Spirit of God (1 Corinthians 2:12)

- The love of God (Romans 5:5)

- Righteousness, peace, and joy (Romans 14:17)

- The mind of Christ (1 Corinthians 2:16)

I can...

- Do all things through Christ who strengthens me (Philippians 4:13).

Though we may often feel the drain and strain of life, may we ever look to the One who said,

> *"Fear not, for I am with you;*
> *Be not dismayed, for I am your God.*
> *I will strengthen you,*
> *Yes, I will help you,*
> *I will uphold you with My righteous right hand."*
>
> Isaiah 41:10

Chapter 15

SHARING GRACE

As base a thing as money often is, yet it can be transmuted into everlasting treasure. It can be converted into food for the hungry and clothing for the poor. It can keep a missionary actively winning lost men to the light of the gospel and thus transmute itself into heavenly values. Any temporal possession can be turned into everlasting wealth. Whatever is given to Christ is immediately touched with immortality.

—A.W. Tozer[1]

God is the source of every blessing. Initially, we are the recipients of His gracious benevolence, but the desire of our heart should then be for God to also make us distributors of His provisions. This is true not only of God's spiritual blessings in our lives, but also of the natural provisions and blessings in our lives. It is important to understand that God's grace applies to the natural needs of our lives as well as the spiritual needs.

And God is able to make all grace (every favor and earthly blessing) come to you in abundance, so that you may always and under all circumstances and whatever the need be self-sufficient [possessing enough to require no aid or support and furnished in abundance for every good work and charitable donation].

2 Corinthians 9:8 AMP

- Sharing grace is God's power and ability to meet our needs and make us joyful in giving to others.

- Sharing grace keeps us from lack and selfishness.

- Sharing grace is the impartation of God's generosity.

- Sharing grace is Love Supplying.

In contemplating how to present sharing grace, I was reminded of an early lesson I learned about Bible interpretation. There is not only a "road of truth," but there is a ditch on either side of the road. Both ditches represent distorting the truth into extreme, excess, or error. When it comes to the issue of money, it seems there is a huge ditch on either side of the road! Some people believe money should never be discussed from the pulpit or in church, while others seem to be totally obsessed with money, almost to the exclusion of all other topics.

My desire is to avoid both ditches and to stay in the middle of the road. Money is frequently discussed throughout the Old Testament, in the teachings of Jesus, in the book of Acts, and by the writers of New Testament epistles. The Word teaches us how to have a healthy and holy attitude toward money and material things. The Word also issues many warnings about the pitfalls of pursuing riches or trusting in riches.

> *Command those who are rich in this present age not to be haughty, nor to trust in uncertain riches but in the living God, who gives us richly all things to enjoy. Let them do good, that they be rich in good works, ready to give, willing to share.*
>
> 1 Timothy 6:17-18

When greed, covetousness, deception, and pride have been stripped away, there remains the beautiful truth in Scripture that God blesses people.

Love Supplying

God is love, and from His love comes every other blessing. We have seen that His grace is an outward expression, a tangible act of His love for us; and so it follows that sharing grace is part of His expression of love. In fact, giving is the first attribute of God's love we see as believers. Verse after verse of Scripture portrays giving as the consequential outflow of love.

- "For God so loved the world that He gave..." (John 3:16).

- "The life which I now live in the flesh I live by faith in the Son of God, who loved me and gave Himself for me" (Galatians 2:20).

- "...as Christ also has loved us and given Himself for us" (Ephesians 5:2).

- "...just as Christ also loved the church and gave Himself for her" (Ephesians 5:25).

- "Now may our Lord Jesus Christ Himself, and our God and Father, who has loved us and given us everlasting consolation and good hope by grace..." (2 Thessalonians 2:16).

The spiritual blessings God has given us are amazing and wonderful, but His blessings are not merely spiritual. God created the material, natural realm as well, and He cares about meeting the needs of His children. It has often been said that God doesn't mind us having things; He just doesn't want things to "have us."

> *For the Lord God is a sun and shield;*
>
> *The Lord will give grace and glory;*
>
> *No good thing will He withhold*
>
> *From those who walk uprightly.*

Psalm 84:11

"But seek first the kingdom of God and His righteousness, and all these things shall be added to you."

Matthew 6:33

"Therefore I say to you, all things for which you pray and ask, believe that you have received them, and they shall be granted you."

Mark 11:24 NASB

It's Okay to Enjoy Things

God says in 1 Timothy 6:17 that He "gives us richly all things to enjoy." He doesn't want us to be prideful, selfish, or have misplaced trust, and He also desires that we be generous and share our resources freely; but most of all, He doesn't want us to miss the part where we enjoy the things He has blessed us with. Don't feel guilty about enjoying what you have!

> *The blessing of the LORD makes one rich,*
>
> *And He adds no sorrow with it.*

Proverbs 10:22

In the first few years of my marriage to Lisa, a teenager in the youth group admired her guitar and asked how she had obtained such a nice instrument. In a half-humorous way, Lisa told him that her Father owned the cattle on a thousand hills. The next week the boy came to me and said, "Tell me more about that ranch your wife's dad owns." I smiled and told him Lisa was referring to Psalm 50:10, and then I encouraged him that God likes to bless all of His children.

There is nothing more pleasurable to a parent than giving something to their child, watching that child jump for joy over the gift, and then immediately begin enjoying it. If we as natural parents love giving good things to our children, how much more does our Heavenly Father enjoy blessing us—and seeing us enjoy what He has given! Jesus said,

You are wrong, and yet you know how to give good things to your children. Much more, your Father in Heaven will give good things to those who ask him.

Matthew 7:11 we

Some may think that the warning in 1 Timothy 6:17-18 that says, "Command those who are rich in this present age not to be haughty, nor to trust in uncertain riches," does not apply to them because they are not rich. However, being rich in one nation is different from being rich in another. To the average African in the Sudan, the poor in America are rich.

Depending on which statistics you look at, it is estimated that nearly half of the world's population lives on less than $2.50 a day, and at least 80 percent of people on the Earth live on less than $10 a day.[2] It may be that you are facing difficult financial challenges at this moment, but that is subject to change. I believe God has given you potential you have never realized, potential ideas you have yet to discover, and promises that are worth fighting for.

Regardless of where you are economically, whether you consider yourself well supplied with abundant possessions or struggling and barely making it, God's sharing grace is extended to you, and He wants to work in your life.

God's Sharing Grace Is Ready to Meet You!

In Galatians 2:10, Paul recalled his promise to the Jerusalem church leaders that he would "remember the poor." He had the opportunity to fulfill his promise by coordinating a special relief offering for believers in Judea who had become impoverished through persecution and famine.

As Paul encouraged the Corinthians to participate in this offering, he linked the concept of grace with giving and generosity. He was appealing to God's love and generosity on the inside of them, hoping to see it manifest in their hearts and lives toward others.

> *Moreover, brethren, we make known to you* **the grace of God** *bestowed on the churches of Macedonia: that in a great trial of affliction the abundance of their joy and their deep poverty abounded in* **the riches of their liberality**. *For I bear witness that according to their ability, yes, and beyond their ability, they were freely willing, imploring us with much urgency that we would receive* **the gift and the fellowship of the ministering to the saints**. *And not only as we had hoped, but they first gave themselves to the Lord, and then to us by the will of God. So we urged Titus, that as he had begun, so he would also complete* **this grace** *in you as well. But as you abound in everything—in faith, in speech, in knowledge, in all diligence, and in your love for us—see that you abound in* **this grace** *also.*
>
> *I speak not by commandment, but I am testing the sincerity of your love by the diligence of others. For you know* **the grace of our Lord Jesus Christ**, *that though He was rich, yet for your sakes He became poor, that you through His poverty might become rich.*
>
> 2 Corinthians 8:1-9 (bold mine)

Paul clearly presents giving as grace-motivated and grace-energized. He is talking to the Corinthian believers in southern Greece, and he refers to the sharing grace of God operating in the Macedonian believers and Jesus. I believe he used these two examples of sharing grace to inspire the Corinthians. The Macedonians had not waited until they became millionaires before giving generously. Paul said their gracious generosity originated in the midst of "a great trial of affliction" and in the midst of "deep poverty." Of course, most people would expect their giving to be "meager," but Paul referred to it as "the riches of their liberality."

You may remember the church in Smyrna that Jesus spoke to in Revelation 2:9 NLT. He said, "I know about your suffering and your poverty—but you are rich!" These verses seem paradoxical. How can the believers in Macedonia and Smyrna both be described as generous and rich in spite of their poverty? Jesus said in Luke 12:15, "One's life does not consist in the abundance of the things he possesses."

Grace was operating so much in the Corinthians that they were not stingy or miserly. As a result, they did far more than Paul expected. Today people say that if they come into a huge sum of money they will become big givers, but that is not necessarily true. If a person is not generous with the little bit they have, they probably won't become generous if they acquire a large amount of money.

If you are faithful in little things, you will be faithful in large ones. But if you are dishonest in little things, you won't be honest with greater responsibilities. And if you are untrustworthy about worldly wealth, who will trust you with the true riches of heaven? And if you are not faithful with other people's things, why should you be trusted with things of your own?

Luke 16:10-12 NLT

Sharing grace gives freely, generously, and cheerfully, and God measures the gift by the heart, not simply by the amount.

And He looked up and saw the rich putting their gifts into the treasury, and He saw also a certain poor widow putting in two mites. So He said, "Truly I say to you that this poor widow has put in more than all; for all these out of their abundance have put in offerings for God, but she out of her poverty put in all the livelihood that she had."

Luke 21:1-4

Let's consider some of Paul's additional admonitions to the Corinthians about their participation in the offering for the struggling saints in Judea.

Remember this—a farmer who plants only a few seeds will get a small crop. But the one who plants generously will get a generous crop. You must each decide in your heart how much to give. And don't give reluctantly or in response to pressure. "For **God loves a person who gives cheerfully."** *And* **God will generously provide all you need. Then you will always have everything you need and plenty left over to share with others.** *As the Scriptures say,*

"They share freely and give generously *to the poor.*

Their good deeds will be remembered forever."

For God is the one who provides seed for the farmer and then bread to eat. In the same way, **he will provide and increase your resources and then produce a great harvest of generosity in you.**

Yes, **you will be enriched in every way so that you can always be generous.** *And when we take your gifts to those who need them, they will thank God. So two good things will result from this ministry of giving—the needs of the believers in Jerusalem will be met, and they will joyfully express their thanks to God.*

As a result of your ministry, they will give glory to God. For **your generosity** *to them and to all believers will prove that you are obedient to the Good News of Christ. And they will pray for you with deep affection because of* **the overflowing grace God has given to you.**

2 Corinthians 9:6-14 NLT (bold mine)

Wow! After all of these fantastic statements about cheerfulness, sowing and reaping, increase, and generosity, Paul says that the source of all these things was "the overflowing grace" God had given to the Corinthians.

> Grace is first a quality of graciousness in the Giver, and then a quality of gratitude in the recipient, which in turn makes him gracious to those around.
>
> —W. H. Griffith Thomas[3]

Wisdom from Proverbs

Throughout the book of Proverbs, great instruction is given to help us live in sharing grace, receiving God's provisions and releasing them toward others.

Let love and faithfulness never leave you;
bind them around your neck,
write them on the tablet of your heart.
Then you will win favor and a good name
in the sight of God and man.

Proverbs 3:3-4 NIV

Honor the LORD with your possessions,
And with the firstfruits of all your increase;
So your barns will be filled with plenty,
And your vats will overflow with new wine.

Proverbs 3:9-10

The hand of the diligent makes rich.

Proverbs 10:4

The labor of the righteous leads to life.

Proverbs 10:16

There is one who scatters, yet increases more;
And there is one who withholds more than is right,
But it leads to poverty.
The generous soul will be made rich,
And he who waters will also be watered himself.

Proverbs 11:24-25

The hand of the diligent will rule.

Proverbs 12:24

He who gathers by labor will increase.

Proverbs 13:11

The godly love to give!

Proverbs 21:26 NLT

By humility and the fear of the LORD
Are riches and honor and life.

Proverbs 22:4

He who has a generous eye will be blessed,
For he gives of his bread to the poor.

Proverbs 22:9

A hard worker has plenty of food,
but a person who chases fantasies ends up in poverty.
The trustworthy person will get a rich reward,
but a person who wants quick riches will get into trouble.

Proverbs 28:19-20 NLT

Trusting the LORD leads to prosperity.

Proverbs 28:25 NLT

Whoever gives to the poor will lack nothing,
but those who close their eyes to poverty will be cursed.

Proverbs 28:27 NLT

In addition to the examples cited above, Proverbs is loaded with God's wisdom concerning every area of life. All of these work hand-in-glove with God's sharing grace and enable us to live a life that is both enriched by God and a blessing to others.

Notice the reference to labor in the verses from Proverbs. Sharing grace operates in conjunction with a good work ethic, not against it. Some who possess a strong work ethic think God's grace had nothing to do with the prosperity they walk in. It was their hard work that brought them material provision and blessing. If that is you, remember whose air you breathe, where your brain cells came from, and who gave you favor, talent, and wisdom!

In a general sense, there is a graciousness that God has extended to all humanity, saved and unsaved alike, in that He created a place for us that was "very good" (Genesis 1:31), a beautiful Earth that sustains us today. Though we work, God is still the provider and deserves the glory and honor.

Beautiful Givers

Were the whole realm of nature mine,
That were an offering far too small;
Love so amazing, so divine,
Demands my soul, my life, my all.

—Isaac Watts

This beautiful hymn says it all! And no doubt, if the apostle Paul were to have known it, he would think of the Philippians. He had established relationships with several churches, but none of his letters expresses a greater sense of affection, appreciation, and brotherly warmth than his epistle to the Philippians. Not only did they help the impoverished saints in Jerusalem, they alone provided regular financial support for Paul and his ministry.

In Philippians 1:5 NLT Paul said, "You have been my partners in spreading the Good News about Christ from the time you first heard it until now." The Amplified Bible renders that verse, "[I thank my God] for your fellowship (your sympathetic cooperation and contributions and partnership) in advancing the good news (the Gospel)." In verse 7 he went on to say, "It is right for me to think this of you all, because I have you in my heart...you all are partakers with me of grace."

The relationship between Paul and the Philippians was rooted in a spiritual connection of grace that was expressed through monetary support. They didn't just "do giving;" they were "giving people." They lived in the reality of God's sharing grace. Such giving from the heart (not from compulsion, guilt, pressure, or manipulation) energizes both givers and recipients and expresses the beauty of grace.

How I praise the Lord that you are concerned about me again. I know you have always been concerned for me, but you didn't have the chance to help me. Not that I was ever in need, for I have learned how to be content with whatever I have. I know how to live on almost nothing or with everything. I have learned the secret of living in every situation, whether it is with a full stomach or empty, with plenty or little. For I can do everything through Christ, who gives me strength. Even so, you have done well to share with me in my present difficulty.

As you know, you Philippians were the only ones who gave me financial help when I first brought you the Good News and then traveled on from Macedonia. No other church did this. Even when I was in Thessalonica you sent help more than once. I don't say this because I want a gift from you. Rather, I want you to receive a reward for your kindness.

At the moment I have all I need—and more! I am generously supplied with the gifts you sent me with Epaphroditus. They are a sweet-smelling sacrifice that is acceptable and pleasing to God. And this same God who takes care of me will supply all your needs from his glorious riches, which have been given to us in Christ Jesus.

Philippians 4:10-19 NLT

Many believers paraphrase Philippians 4:19, "My God shall supply all my needs," without appreciating the depth of sharing grace that existed in the relationship between these precious believers and Paul. Their love for him and their respect for his ministry motivated their giving, and Paul said their giving was, "a sweet-smelling sacrifice that is acceptable and pleasing to God." This is why the Philippians were beautiful givers.

If you want to be a beautiful giver, check your motives. If you give grudgingly, under compulsion, or because of guilt, your giving is not grace-based. There are great benefits to giving, but those benefits are not unqualified or automatically received. Consider the radical statement made by Paul in 1 Corinthians 13:3: "And though I bestow all my goods to feed the poor, and though I give my body to be burned, but have not love, it profits me nothing." Grace-based giving is never based on the question, "What will I get out of this?" If you really want to be partners with the God of all grace and give like He gives, then you need to give with the same motivation He gives—love.

The woman who anointed Jesus with a costly flask of perfume just prior to His death did what Jesus said was "a good work," and He was not the least bit bothered that the value of this perfume was equivalent to a year's wages. Judas and others were angry at the "waste," but instead of sharing in their indignation, Jesus said,

"Let her alone. Why do you trouble her? She has done a good work for Me. For you have the poor with you always, and whenever you wish you may do them good; but Me you do not have always. She has done what she could. She has come beforehand to anoint My body for burial. Assuredly, I say to you, wherever this gospel is preached in the whole world, what this woman has done will also be told as a memorial to her."

Mark 14:6-9

Jesus was not uptight about money. In this account, He expressed appreciation for the gift the woman bestowed upon Him, and He drew attention to the fact that, "She has done what she could." There was something about this that truly touched Jesus' heart. This woman's giving was not mechanical or obligatory; it came from her heart, and Jesus honored her for it.

Barnabas is another example of a beautiful giver:

And Joses, who was also named Barnabas by the apostles (which is translated Son of Encouragement)...having land, sold it, and brought the money and laid it at the apostles' feet.

Acts 4:36-37

The apostles in Jerusalem were greatly impressed with the generous heart of Barnabas, who later became an apostle himself. Then a couple named Ananias and Sapphira deceptively tried to emulate Barnabas' act of graciousness. They paid a dear price for their dishonesty and wrong motives. Peter confronted them and they died for lying to the Holy Spirit. People see what we do, but God knows why we are doing it. A beautiful giver has an honest heart of love.

Though not necessarily a person of great financial means, Dorcas of Joppa was a beautiful giver. Acts 9:36 NLT says, "She was always doing kind things for others and helping the poor." When she died, Peter came. Acts 9:39 NLT says, "The room was filled with widows who were weeping and showing him the coats and other clothes Dorcas had made for them." Peter raised her from the dead, and that was a great miracle, but don't overlook the tremendous blessing she was to others. The beauty of her generosity had touched many hearts and lives.

Beautiful sharing grace emerges in the most unusual places. A survivor of a Nazi concentration camp told this remarkable story:

Ilse, a childhood friend of mine, once found a raspberry in the concentration camp and carried it in her pocket all day to present to me that night on a leaf. Imagine a world in which your entire possession is one raspberry and you give it to your friend.

—Gerda Weissmann Klein[4]

Pastor Eric Hulstrand from Binford, North Dakota, related another story of beautiful giving:

While I was preaching one Sunday, an elderly woman, Mary, fainted and struck her head on the end of the pew. Immediately, an EMT in the congregation called an ambulance. As they strapped her to a stretcher and got ready to head out the door, Mary regained consciousness. She motioned for her daughter to come near. Everyone thought she was summoning her strength to convey what could be her final words. The daughter leaned over until her ear was at her mother's mouth. "My offering is in my purse," she whispered.[5]

A beautiful giver I know personally is Carolyn Zumwalt. She and her husband Claude were Sunday school teachers at the church where Lisa and I served as janitors during our first year of Bible school. We were newly married and they took us under their wing, showing us much kindness. Claude went home to be with the Lord in 2006, and Carolyn found great help and comfort from my book, *Life After Death*. At the time of this writing, she has purchased and given away more than three hundred and thirty copies to help others deal with grief.

It's been amazing how the Lord has directed my path to people in need of your book. Then they come back and tell what a blessing it has been to them. One lady told me she'd read the book five times. Many have said the book was "exactly what they needed." I met a lady today at Wal-Mart who had just lost her daughter. I reached in my purse and handed her your book. I led a grief recovery group twice at my church and I gave each person one of your books. They all agreed it was such a blessing to their lives. When people offer to pay me for the book, I refuse. Thank you so much for writing this book.

—Carolyn Zumwalt

As a beautiful giver, Carolyn has been fulfilling 2 Corinthians 1:3-4:

The Father of mercies and God of all comfort...comforts us in all our tribulation, that we may be able to comfort those who are in any trouble, with the comfort with which we ourselves are comforted by God.

Sharing Grace Abounded in Jesus' Life

The Lord Jesus, of course, is our ultimate example of a beautiful giver. He was full of grace (John 1:14), the grace of God was upon Him (Luke 2:40), and of course, He gave His life for us. However, God's power was at work in His life meeting His needs and enabling Him to cheerfully meet the needs of others. Religious tradition has portrayed Jesus as impoverished, but the Gospels reveal a different picture.

Luke 2:52 says, "Jesus increased in wisdom and stature, and in favor with God and men." The Message renders this, "And Jesus matured, growing up in both body and spirit, blessed by both God and people." These blessings included financial provision. There were many ways God provided for Him. When the wise men from the East arrived, Matthew 2:11 NLT tells us, "They bowed down and worshiped him. Then they opened their treasure chests and gave him gifts of gold, frankincense, and myrrh." They were wealthy men who brought gifts fit for a king. These gifts were likely the resources that enabled Joseph to take his young family to Egypt when Herod threatened to kill the young Jesus. This treasure could have also sustained them until Herod died and they could return to Israel.

In His ministry, Jesus and His team had ministry partners who provided them with regular financial support. Luke 8:2-3 NCV mentions many women, "who used their own money to help Jesus and his apostles." Jesus was so blessed financially that in Luke 22:35 He declared His disciples had never lacked anything during their time with Him, even when He sent them out to minister. Furthermore, He was given so much that He appointed a treasurer.

> *But Judas did not really care about the poor; he said this because he was a thief. He was the one who kept the money box, and he often stole from it.*
>
> John 12:6 NCV

When Judas left the Passover meal to betray Jesus, the other disciples assumed he had gone to make a purchase or to give something to the poor (John 13:29). Apparently, those types of transactions were common for Judas. Even though Judas regularly embezzled funds from the ministry, there was still enough money for regular purchases and giving to the poor. This does not sound like what happens in the life of an impoverished man, does it?

Even in death Jesus had benefactors: Joseph of Arimathea and Nicodemus. Matthew 27:57-60 NLT tells us that Joseph was a rich man who requested the body of Jesus from Pilate, prepared it for burial, and "placed it in his own new tomb, which had been carved out of rock." John 19:39 NLT informs us Nicodemus joined Joseph in helping prepare Jesus' body for burial, and that he "brought seventy-five pounds of perfumed ointment made from myrrh and aloes." William Barclay wrote, "Nicodemus brought enough spices for the burial of a king."[6] The New American Commentary says, "It was truly an immense amount of spice. Indeed, it was enough spice to bury a king royally."[7]

I am not implying that Jesus lived lavishly while on Earth. There are no accounts of Him riding around in a golden chariot or living in opulence, but His needs were met generously and He often met the needs of others. Certainly the outflow of sharing grace that came from the heart and life of Jesus—and still comes to us today—makes Him the most beautiful giver of all.

Principles of Giving

Here are some principles from the New Testament on how we are to operate in sharing grace:

Believers are to give PERSONALLY. In 2 Corinthians 8:1-5, Paul described the great generosity of the Macedonians, and he said (verse 5), "They first gave themselves to the Lord, and then to us by the will of God." Our giving is not just a religious ritual, but it reflects a life totally given to God. Giving is to be from the heart, the core of who we are.

Believers are to give SYSTEMATICALLY. Paul said in 1 Corinthians 16:2, "On the first day of the week let each one of you lay something aside." Systematic and regular giving produces stability in churches and promotes maturity, discipline, and responsibility in believers. When God's sharing grace is prevalent in our lives, it produces consistency in our giving.

Believers are to give PROPORTIONATELY. First Corinthians 16:2 also says, "On the first day of the week let each one of you lay something aside, storing up as he may prosper." Giving is to be in proportion to how much we prosper.

Believers are to give GENEROUSLY. Proverbs 11:25 says, "The generous soul will be made rich, And he who waters will also be watered himself." Keep in mind this doesn't just apply to money. We can also be generous with our time, our talents, and our encouragement of others. Romans 12:8 refers to those who give "with liberality."

Believers are to give WILLINGLY. In Exodus 35:5 Moses said, "Take from among you an offering to the LORD. Whoever is of a willing heart, let him bring it as an offering to the LORD." Isaiah 1:19 says, "If you are willing and obedient, You shall eat the good of the land."

Believers are to give PURPOSEFULLY. One of my favorite verses on giving has always been 2 Corinthians 9:7, which says, "So let each one give as he purposes in his heart." Giving should be deliberate and intentional not because of pressure, hype, manipulation, or to impress others.

Believers are to give CHEERFULLY. The last part of 2 Corinthians 9:7 says, "God loves a cheerful giver." The word "cheerful" is the Greek word *hilaros*, from which we get our English word "hilarious."[7] Giving truly should be a joy! The Amplified version of verse 7 reads: "God loves (He takes pleasure in, prizes above other things, and is unwilling to abandon or to do without) a cheerful (joyous, "prompt to do it") giver [whose heart is in his giving]."

Believers are to give RESPONSIBLY. There is a principle of responsibility when it comes to finances. We are to faithfully support our local church and do our part in carrying out the Great Commission (Matthew 28:19-20). The Moravian Covenant for Christian Living says, "We deem it a sacred responsibility and genuine opportunity to be faithful stewards of all God has entrusted to us: our time, our talents, and our financial resources. We view all of life as a sacred trust to be used wisely."[9]

Believers are to give EXPECTANTLY. Many scriptures, such as Ecclesiastes 11:1-3 and Luke 6:38, address the blessing connected with giving, and we should give with a heart of expectancy.

Believers are to give WORSHIPFULLY. True giving is far more than a financial transaction; it is an act of worship unto God. Deuteronomy 26:10-11 instructs, "Then you shall set it before the LORD your God, and worship before the LORD your God. So you shall rejoice in every good thing which the LORD your God has given to you and your house."

Believers with mature attitudes toward material things and money are deeply impacted by God's sharing grace. Such individuals have come to an understanding that everything is God's, and that He has simply allowed them to be stewards for a season. Spirit-led, grace-motivated Christians are not examining the Bible to see how little they can give and still be okay with God; rather, they have consecrated themselves and everything they have entirely to God. They also know that because of their covenant with God, all that He has is theirs.

With this understanding of kingdom economics, they are committed to using the resources God has entrusted to them to help advance His kingdom and glorify Him. Instead of seeing how little they can give, they are prayerfully seeking how much they can give and where they are to give.

> I place no value on anything I have or may possess, except in relation to the kingdom of God. If anything will advance the interests of the kingdom, it shall be given away or kept, only as by giving or keeping it I shall most promote the glory of Him to whom I owe all my hopes in time or eternity.
>
> —David Livingstone[10]

Is Tithing for New Testament Believers?

The word "tithe" is an older word that simply means "tenth" (as in one-tenth, or 10 percent).[11] Old Testament saints understood the tithe to be a tenth of their financial increase or income, given to God as an expression of faith and consecration. Tithing is addressed as early as the book of Genesis and remains a topic of interest, discussion, and debate today.

There are various opinions from good people on all sides of the tithing issue. Some reject the tithe as mandatory for New Testament believers, claiming that it was an Old Testament practice associated with the Law. Others believe the tithe remains a vital expression of faith and obedience. They deem it a timeless principle that transcends all covenants.

Even though tithing began well before the time of Moses, many regulations were applied to tithing by the Law when it came, and many of these stipulations reflected their farming society. If you study the Mosaic Law in-depth, some of the statements about the tithe would be difficult for most people to apply today because of all the references to animals, grain, and other agricultural requirements. Here are a few of the references to tithing under the Mosaic Law:

> *And all the tithe of the land, whether of the seed of the land or of the fruit of the tree, is the LORD's. It is holy to the LORD.*
>
> Leviticus 27:30

> *You shall truly tithe all the increase of your grain that the field produces year by year.*
>
> Deuteronomy 14:22

> *As soon as the commandment was circulated, the children of Israel brought in abundance the firstfruits of grain and wine, oil and honey, and of all the produce of the field; and they brought in abundantly the tithe of everything. And the children of Israel and Judah, who dwelt in the cities of Judah, brought the tithe of oxen and sheep; also the tithe of holy things which were consecrated to the LORD their God they laid in heaps.*
>
> 2 Chronicles 31:5-6

> *Then all Judah brought the tithe of the grain and the new wine and the oil to the storehouse.*
>
> Nehemiah 13:12

"Will a man rob God?

Yet you have robbed Me!

But you say,

'In what way have we robbed You?'

In tithes and offerings.

> *You are cursed with a curse,*

For you have robbed Me,

Even this whole nation.

> *Bring all the tithes into the storehouse,*

That there may be food in My house,

And try Me now in this,"

Says the Lord of hosts,

"If I will not open for you the windows of heaven

And pour out for you such blessing

That there will not be room enough to receive it.

> *"And I will rebuke the devourer for your sakes,*

So that he will not destroy the fruit of your ground,

Nor shall the vine fail to bear fruit for you in the field,"

Says the Lord of hosts.

Malachi 3:8-11

Jesus first mentioned tithing when he contrasted a self-righteous, self-justifying man with a man who acknowledged his sinfulness and appealed to the mercy of God (Luke 18:9-14). Tithing, along with fasting and avoiding certain sins, was the basis for the first man's sense of pride and self-reliance. Jesus did not say tithing, fasting, or avoiding sin is wrong, merely that those things should not produce pride, haughtiness, and self-righteousness.

Jesus' second reference to tithing occurred when He was speaking to religious leaders. He said,

"What sorrow awaits you teachers of religious law and you Pharisees. Hypocrites! For you are careful to tithe even the tiniest income from your herb gardens, but you ignore the more important aspects of the law—justice, mercy, and faith. You should tithe, yes, but do not neglect the more important things."

Matthew 23:23 NLT

Jesus acknowledged tithing as a good thing; it was a part of the Law. However, He also pointed out that hyper-technical tithing should not be used to establish a spiritual superiority complex, nor should tithing cause us to overlook or ignore God's nature of justice, mercy, and faith. Jesus said these were more important aspects of the Law.

Those who believe tithing has become obsolete in the New Covenant point out that we are no longer under the Law, but tithing did not originate with the Law. The first instance of tithing was a spontaneous action of faith and consecration on the part of Abraham.

Then Melchizedek king of Salem brought out bread and wine; he was the priest of God Most High. And he blessed him and said
Blessed be Abram of God Most High,
> *Possessor of heaven and earth;*
And blessed be God Most High,
> *Who has delivered your enemies into your hand."*
And he gave him a tithe of all.

Genesis 14:18-20

Melchizedek was a type or prophetic foreshadowing of the Lord Jesus Christ, our Great High Priest. Some believe Melchizedek was a pre-Bethlehemic manifestation of the Son of God. In Hebrews 7, we learn that the priesthood of Melchizedek was not like the Levitical priesthood, which was connected to the Law of Moses and eventually discontinued. Jesus, our Great High Priest, is a different kind of priest altogether.

This change has been made very clear since a different priest, who is like Melchizedek, has appeared. Jesus became a priest, not by meeting the physical requirement of belonging to the tribe of Levi, but by the power of a life that cannot be destroyed. And the psalmist pointed this out when he prophesied,

"You are a priest forever in the order of Melchizedek."

Yes, the old requirement about the priesthood was set aside because it was weak and useless. For the law never made anything perfect. But now we have confidence in a better hope, through which we draw near to God.

Hebrews 7:15-19 NLT

In Hebrews 8:6, we learn that Jesus "has obtained a more excellent ministry, inasmuch as He is also Mediator of a better covenant, which was established on better promises." This verse teaches the superiority of Jesus' priesthood, which is patterned after the priesthood of Melchizedek. This means Jesus is the Priest who receives our tithes.

Abraham encountered Melchizedek one time, and he paid him tithes; our High Priest lives in us and we live in Him. Therefore, it should not seem strange to tithe to the Lord as a part of our lifestyle. Romans 4:12 and 16 refer to those, "who also walk in the steps of the faith which our father Abraham had," and "those who are of the faith of Abraham, who is the father of us all."

New Covenant believers are not under the Mosaic Law of the tithe, but there is a principle of the tithe (an expression of faith and consecration) that remains for us. We present our tithe to the Lord Jesus Christ just as Abraham presented his tithe to Melchizedek. If we believe that our High Priest, Jesus, really is the Mediator of a better covenant established upon better promises (Hebrews 8:6), would we want to do less "under grace" than Old Testament believers did "under law?" Their tithes supplied provision for the priesthood and the Temple, and that was important. But our tithes provide for the work of the Church and the proclamation of the gospel which affect the souls of men for eternity. Such work deserves our best!

Put God First

"But seek first the kingdom of God and His righteousness, and all these things shall be added to you."

Matthew 6:33

This statement of Jesus is such a vital and powerful truth, and yet there are so many Christians who still throw one dollar into the offering plate each week, knowing they could give much more. I find it troubling that most churches are operating on a mere fraction of what they could be operating on if all Christians at least gave a tenth of their income to those who labored to feed them spiritually.

Think what would happen in and through the Body of Christ if all Christians decided to honor God and to put God first in their finances. What if every Christian decided to honor God with the tithe (10% of his or her income) and then planned their budget to live on the remaining 90% of their income? The income of many churches would multiply greatly, God's people would be enormously blessed, and the proclamation of the gospel could be abundantly funded and underwritten.

Unfortunately, many Christians are struggling financially and in excessive debt. Some have experienced hardships that were beyond their control, while others have over-extended themselves through ill-advised spending. American culture promotes self-indulgence, self-gratification, and greed—well facilitated by our credit system (I am not against credit used wisely, but so many abuse credit and end up in trouble). More importantly, instead of having an intimate relationship with God in their finances, following His counsel and instructions, many act independently. They buy what they want, do the things they want to do—and if something is left over, then maybe it will go to God.

In a *Christianity Today* article entitled "Scrooge Lives," Rob Moll wrote,

> More than one out of four American Protestants give away no money at all—"not even a token $5 per year," say sociologists Christian Smith, Michael Emerson, and Patricia Snell in a new study on Christian giving, Passing the Plate (Oxford University Press). Of all Christian groups, evangelical Protestants score best: only 10 percent give nothing away. Evangelicals tend to be the most generous, but they do not outperform their peers enough to wear a badge of honor. Thirty-six percent report that they give away less than two percent of their income. Only about 27 percent tithe.[12]

These believers are missing the directive Jesus gave: seek first God's kingdom!

If you are struggling financially and have never tithed, none of this is meant to be condemning. God is for you not against you. His love for you is not based on how much money you give to His work, but God wants to be involved in your finances, and that includes both giving and receiving.

It is good for you, your church, and others if you get God's wisdom about your finances and become a generous, beautiful giver like Him, like Jesus, like Barnabas, and like the woman who poured an entire year's wages in perfume on the feet of Jesus. This may involve developing a biblical world-view and entirely recalibrating your value system, but the benefits are amazing.

You will know God's sharing grace has done a great work in your heart when you no longer see tithing or giving as a grievous burden but as a joyous blessing. Instead of seeing how little you can give, you always look for ways to give generously—in every area of life—because that is the way of sharing grace!

I have shown you in every way, by laboring like this, that you must support the weak. And remember the words of the Lord Jesus, that He said, "It is more blessed to give than to receive."

Acts 20:35

Chapter 16

SERVING GRACE

Paul did not labor in order to receive grace, but he received grace so that he might labor.

—Augustine[1]

S aving, sanctifying, and strengthening grace are predominantly inward workings of God's grace for our benefit. Sharing grace benefits us, but our giving generously benefits others also. Serving grace is given to us predominantly for the benefit of others. I have reserved serving grace for the last of the five expressions of God's grace because it is the wellspring—the fountainhead—of all ministerial gifts, callings, and abilities. It is a divine deposit in our lives from Heaven that enables us to serve God in a way that pleases Him and benefits everyone in our lives.

- Serving grace is God's power and ability to serve Him and others with His divinely imparted gifts and aptitudes.
- Serving grace keeps us from being unproductive.
- Serving grace is the impartation of God's ability.
- Serving grace is Love Assisting.

Paul's Life and Ministry

Paul did far more than teach the doctrine grace; his life was radically transformed by God's saving, sanctifying, and strengthening grace, and his life was governed by God's sharing and serving grace. God's grace saved him, made him more and more Christlike, gave him the ability to endure the hardships of ministry, and made him a beautiful giver. Now we will see how God's serving grace empowered Paul to know and fulfill his calling.

Paul said that through Christ, he had, "received grace and apostleship" (Romans 1:5). He stated that the grace of God had made him a "wise master builder" and enabled him to establish the Corinthian church (1 Corinthians 3:10). Concerning his ministerial and ethical conduct: "We have depended on God's grace, not on our own human wisdom" (2 Corinthians 1:12 NLT). He spoke of the, "dispensation of the grace of God," (Ephesians 3:2) a revelation that God gave to him for believers in Christ, and he "became a minister according to the gift of the grace of God" (Ephesians 3:7). Claiming to be less than the least of all saints, Paul said, "To me...this grace was given, that I should preach...the unsearchable riches of Christ" (Ephesians 3:8).

Paul's message was not generated from his intellect or will. He said, "I say, through the grace given to me..." (Romans 12:3). He understood that the things he spoke and wrote were grace-generated and grace-based. He also told the Roman church, "I have written more boldly to you on some points, as reminding you, because of the grace given to me by God" (Romans 15:15).

Speaking to Timothy, Paul said God had saved and called them "with a holy calling, not according to our works, but according to His own purpose and grace," which had been given to them in Christ before time began (2 Timothy 1:9).

Paul's writings clearly show his appreciation for God's grace in his life and ministry. I think Paul would have agreed with these four statements as well:

- No grace, no salvation.

- No grace, no ministry.

- Saving grace brings mercy and forgiveness to the worst of sinners.

- Serving grace imparts calling and purpose, then empowers and enables us to accomplish them.

Perhaps the most powerful statement Paul ever wrote about the grace of God relative to his own experience is found in 1 Corinthians 15:10:

> *But by the grace of God I am what I am, and His grace toward me was not in vain; but I labored more abundantly than they all, yet not I, but the grace of God which was with me.*

Let's look at the four parts of this verse in detail:

1. By the grace of God I am what I am. Paul's life had undergone a complete transformation by the grace of God. In the verse before this statement (1 Corinthians 15:9), he referenced his pre-Christian life, "I am the least of the apostles, who am not worthy to be called an apostle, because I persecuted the church of God." By modern definitions, Paul (Saul of Tarsus) had been a terrorist. He was viciously persecuting followers of Jesus.

> *Saul shamefully treated and laid waste the church continuously [with cruelty and violence]; and entering house after house, he dragged out men and women and committed them to prison.*
>
> Acts 8:3 AMP

> *I used to blaspheme the name of Christ. In my insolence, I persecuted his people.*
>
> 1 Timothy 1:13 NLT

Other translations describe Saul of Tarsus as an arrogant man, a violent aggressor, shamefully and outrageously and aggressively insulting, an insolent overbearing man, a violent man, a destructive person, and injurious. Though he was clearly mindful of the depth and magnitude of his pre-conversion sin, Paul glorified the God of grace, who forgave him and called him to serve.

> *...although I was formerly a blasphemer, a persecutor, and an insolent man; but I obtained mercy because I did it ignorantly in unbelief. And the grace of our Lord was exceedingly abundant, with faith and love which are in Christ Jesus.*

1 Timothy 1:13-14

When Saul of Tarsus met Jesus, the grace of God did an amazing and revolutionary work in his life. He was transformed:

- from being Saul a hater of Christ to Paul a lover of Christ,
- from being Saul the destroyer to Paul the builder,
- from being an apostle of terror to an apostle of grace.

The change Paul experienced was not cosmetic or superficial; he was transformed from the very core of his being. The full context of, "By the grace of God I am what I am," however, concerns his ministerial assignment. Elsewhere Paul declares, "Even before I was born, God chose me and called me by his marvelous grace" (Galatians 1:15 NLT), and he had been "appointed a preacher, an apostle, and a teacher of the Gentiles" (2 Timothy 1:11). God's grace not only determined Paul's personal identity in Christ, but also his ministerial assignment.

2. His grace toward me was not in vain. Paul reveals the functional nature of serving grace. God's grace must be expressed! It is not empty, wasted, fruitless, worthless, or without purpose. God's grace in Paul produced the desired results in his life and ministry. First Corinthians 15:10 in the Amplified Bible says, "His grace toward me was not [found to be] for nothing (fruitless and without effect)."

3. I labored more abundantly than they all. Paul now contrasts his ministerial labors with that of the other apostles. The New Century Version translates this part of 1 Corinthians 15:10, "I worked harder than all the other apostles." In the Greek this means, "to labor, to work to the point of exhaustion, to work hard...weariness which follows this straining of all his powers to the utmost."[2]

While ministry is rooted in grace, it is still work! "The Holy Spirit said, 'Now separate to Me Barnabas and Saul for the work to which I have called them'" (Acts 13:2). Paul is known as "the Apostle of Grace," but he advocated work and worked diligently himself.

We work wearily with our own hands to earn our living.

1 Corinthians 4:12 NLT

Be steadfast, immovable, always abounding in the work of the Lord, knowing that your labor is not in vain in the Lord.

1 Corinthians 15:58

Timothy...does the work of the Lord, as I also do.

1 Corinthians 16:10

If you are a thief, quit stealing. Instead, use your hands for good hard work, and then give generously to others in need.

Ephesians 4:28 NLT

Don't you remember, dear brothers and sisters, how hard we worked among you? Night and day we toiled to earn a living so that we would not be a burden to any of you as we preached God's Good News to you.

1 Thessalonians 2:9 NLT

...that you also aspire to lead a quiet life, to mind your own business, and to work with your own hands, as we commanded you.

1 Thessalonians 4:11

Apparently the Thessalonians did not grasp the message, because Paul had to address this issue again. He was always compassionate toward those who were truly in need, but he had stern words for individuals who were simply irresponsible and lazy freeloaders.

> *We were not disorderly among you; nor did we eat anyone's bread free of charge, but worked with labor and toil night and day, that we might not be a burden to any of you.*
>
> *For even when we were with you, we commanded you this: If anyone will not work, neither shall he eat. For we hear that there are some who walk among you in a disorderly manner, not working at all, but are busybodies. Now those who are such we command and exhort through our Lord Jesus Christ that they work in quietness and eat their own bread.*
>
> 2 Thessalonians 3:7-8,10-12

Paul had a great understanding of grace, but it did not cause him to put his feet up, kick back, and say, "Thank God that He's done everything. I don't have to do a thing." Grace does not mean we don't work. However, grace influences why we work, how we work, and our attitude toward work. Paul was always mindful that it was God's grace that enabled and empowered him to serve.

4. Yet not I, but the grace of God which was with me. After Paul said he labored tirelessly unto exhaustion, more than any other apostle, he made a dramatic, qualifying statement. "I worked tremendously hard, but it wasn't really me; it was the grace of God with me." That sounds a bit like his statement to the Galatians, "It is no longer I who live, but Christ lives in me" (Galatians 2:20).

Paul worked hard, but he knew he did not labor alone. God's serving grace was being expressed through him. John Chrysostom, the Archbishop of Constantinople who died in 407 A.D., said, "A man's readiness and commitment are not enough if he does not enjoy help from above as well; equally, help from above is no benefit to us unless there is also commitment and readiness on our part."[3]

Co-Laborers in Serving Grace

Paul also recognized the need for co-laborers as he operated in God's serving grace. He said, "I planted, Apollos watered, but God gave the increase. So then neither he who plants is anything, nor he who waters, but God who gives the increase" (1 Corinthians 3:6-7). He went on to say, "We are God's fellow workers" (1 Corinthians 3:9). The Amplified Bible says, "We are fellow workmen (joint promoters, laborers together) with and for God."

Paul recognized the grace of God at work in others. He wrote of the apostle Peter:

> *He Who motivated and fitted Peter and worked effectively through him for the mission to the circumcised, motivated and fitted me and worked through me also for [the mission to] the Gentiles*
>
> Galatians 2:8 AMP

The next verse reads, "When James, Cephas, and John...perceived the grace that had been given to me, they gave me and Barnabas the right hand of fellowship, that we should go to the Gentiles and they to the circumcised" (Galatians 2:9). James, Peter, and John recognized the grace of God that was working in Paul's life.

These verses in Galatians are so descriptive of God's serving grace working in and through Peter and Paul respectively. Paul points out that they had different assignments, and the serving grace they had each received equipped them accordingly. Paul's primary assignment was the Gentiles, while Peter was primarily called to reach Jewish people.

This reveals a foundational principle for operating in God's serving grace: He does not equip you to do someone else's job. Each minister must come to terms with their assignment in ministry. This is why Paul used the phrase, "those things which God has given us to do" (2 Corinthians 10:13 WE). God only gives you grace to serve and be effective in your prescribed field of service.

In Colossians 1:28-29 AMP Paul says that his purpose in ministry was to "present every person mature (full-grown, fully initiated, complete, and perfect) in Christ (the Anointed One). For this I labor [unto weariness], striving with all the superhuman energy which He so mightily enkindles and works within me." Paul labored intensively, but at the end of the day he was quick to acknowledge that the true work and accomplishments were not achieved by his human effort but by the grace of God that was laboring with and through him.

Ministry is not meant to be something we go out and do for God; it is meant to be something we do with God. It is also designed to be a joint-effort with others in Him. As we abide in Him and He abides in us, we are able to serve Him happily and productively. We work, but He is the One who ultimately produces the results by His Word and by His Spirit. That's what serving grace is all about.

Not Just for Preachers

Let us have grace, by which we may serve God acceptably with reverence and godly fear.

Hebrews 12:28

One of the great misconceptions that has plagued the body of Christ for centuries is the idea that paid clergy and "full-time" ministers are the only ones called by God to do the work of the ministry. Some believers have the attitude that when it comes to praying, visitation, encouraging people, evangelism, and all the other aspects of ministry, "That's what we pay the pastor for." Because of this mentality, many church members view themselves as spectators in church services. Simply attending church and sitting in the pew as an observer fulfills their Christian duty. As a result, both they and their churches never achieve their full potential.

The Bible teaches that every born-again believer has some type of calling on their life, an area of service they have been graced by God to fulfill. Peter said:

> *As each one has received a gift, minister it to one another, as good stewards of the manifold grace of God. If anyone speaks, let him speak as the oracles of God. If anyone ministers, let him do it as with the ability which God supplies, that in all things God may be glorified through Jesus Christ, to whom belong the glory and the dominion forever and ever. Amen.*
>
> 1 Peter 4:10-11

> *God has given each of you a gift from his great variety of spiritual gifts. Use them well to serve one another. Do you have the gift of speaking? Then speak as though God himself were speaking through you. Do you have the gift of helping others? Do it with all the strength and energy that God supplies. Then everything you do will bring glory to God through Jesus Christ. All glory and power to him forever and ever! Amen.*
>
> 1 Peter 4:10-11 NLT

Let's note several important points:

Every believer has a gift to use and a function to fulfill. Peter wrote this letter to several congregations, not to preachers. (See 1 Peter 1:1.) He says God gave every believer gifts to use in serving others, and this means that no Christian is to be an inactive spectator or a passive observer.

Believers are to use their gifts to serve one another. Grace is not something God gave us to isolate and remove us from others, but rather, to become better connected with and to become helpful to others. It is very insightful to examine the many times the phrase "one another" is used in the New Testament:

- Love one another (John 13:34; 1 & 2 John, and many more)

- In honor prefer one another (Romans 12:10)

- Receive one another (Romans 15:7)

- Admonish one another (Romans 15:14)

- Serve one another (Galatians 5:13)

- Bear one another's burdens (Galatians 6:2)

- Be kind and tenderhearted to one another (Ephesians 4:32)

- Forgive one another (Ephesians 4:32)

- Teach and admonish one another (Colossians 3:16)

- Increase and abound in love toward one another (1 Thessalonians 3:12)

- Comfort one another (1 Thessalonians 4:18)

- Edify one another (1 Thessalonians 5:11)

- Exhort one another (Hebrews 3:13)

- Confess your faults one to another and pray one for another (James 5:16)

- Be hospitable to one another (1 Peter 4:9)

God desires His people to be communities of love, encouragement, and mutual support. Some of this will occur by individuals serving formally in official positions in the church, while other expressions of His serving grace will flow through us informally and spontaneously in our day-to-day relationships with others. I'm 100% for people serving in their local church, but we don't have to have a title to help, pray, or comfort someone in need.

Believers are to be "good stewards of the manifold grace of God." A steward is someone who manages the affairs or the business of another. In Bible days, a steward did not own his master's property, but he managed it to be the most profitable to the master. Likewise, we are to use our gifts to assist our brothers and sisters in the Lord and promote the kingdom of God, not ourselves. The Greek word translated "manifold" means variegated and many-colored.[4] First Peter 4:10 NLT renders this God's "great variety of spiritual gifts." It should not surprise us that God gifted each person in a unique and special way. If we consider His natural creation, we realize He loves variety. As believers, we are to use the variety of His gifts for the glory of God and the benefit of others.

Two primary expressions of grace are speaking and serving. It would seem the term "manifold" means more than speaking and serving, but Peter emphasizes them. For those whose gift is in the speaking category, in 1 Peter 4:11 he says they are to "speak as the oracles of God." Whether they are an apostle, prophet, evangelist, pastor, or teacher, they are to convey God's Word, not their own opinions, theories, views, and speculations. Those who serve are to do so with the ability, strength, and energy God supplies and are often referred to as "the ministry of helps" (see 1 Corinthians 12:28). *In Search of Timothy—Discovering and Developing Greatness in Church Staff and Volunteers* is a book I wrote especially for those who are called to serve in supportive roles in the Church. Not everyone is called to be in a pulpit ministry! Many more are called to minister behind the scenes.

The glory of God is the result. When those who speak and those who serve are empowered by God's serving grace, He is glorified. We should not speak or serve for attention, ego gratification, or accolades from others. Our service both within the church and outside the church should be based on God's love and directed toward His glory.

The Varieties of Gifts

Discussing the manifold grace of God and covering only speaking and serving is a bit like talking about food and mentioning only fruits and vegetables. Within those two categories are so many! Fruits include bananas, strawberries, apples, and more; vegetables include carrots, peas, broccoli, and more. Speaking and serving can be broken down into more specific lists as well. Paul did exactly that when he addressed the believers in Rome.

> *For I say, through the grace given to me, to everyone who is among you, not to think of himself more highly than he ought to think, but to think soberly, as God has dealt to each one a measure of faith. For as we have many members in one body, but all the members do not have the same function, so we, being many, are one body in Christ, and individually members of one another. Having then gifts differing according to the grace that is given to us, let us use them: if prophecy, let us prophesy in proportion to our faith; or ministry, let us use it in our ministering; he who teaches, in teaching; he who exhorts, in exhortation; he who gives, with liberality; he who leads, with diligence; he who shows mercy, with cheerfulness.*
>
> Romans 12:3-8

Again, the Holy Spirit tells us that grace has not only an individual application but also a corporate application. Just as Peter emphasized "one another," Paul says, "We, being many, are one body in Christ, and individually members of one another" (Romans 12:5). Grace places us into the body of Christ, connects us, and directs us to interact and mutually benefit each other. In this passage in Romans, Paul lists seven ways we can do this that are all functions of serving grace: prophecy, ministry (or serving), teaching, exhorting, giving, leading, and mercy. Here are three things you should know:

1. This list is not exhaustive. These seven expressions of God's grace working through believers are not necessarily the only ways God graces people to serve. For example, Paul mentions hospitality a few verses later in Romans 12:13, as does Peter in 1 Peter 4:9. I believe Paul gave the Romans these seven as a springboard to help them recognize their own gifts for service.

2. This list is not exclusionary. I don't believe God meant for you to lay claim to one of these and then excuse yourself from fulfilling other basic Christian responsibilities. For example, let's say you believe that God has graced you to exhort others. One day you decide you no longer need to support your church financially because you are only called to exhort others. Or if the pastor asks you to visit someone in the hospital, you say, "No, that's not my gift. I only exhort." Then someone offends you and you say, "I don't need to forgive them because mercy isn't my gift." Do you see how foolish this is? Our "gifts" should never exclude us from engaging in basic Christian service or from fulfilling basic Christian responsibilities. We should never say, "Oh, I'm not called to do that," to avoid opportunities of loving and helping others.

3. A person is not necessarily limited to one gift. I believe most individuals have more than one gift. Sometimes these gifts blend together into what might be called a "gift mix," such as mercy and hospitality working together in the life of a believer, or a pastor who functions well in both leading and teaching. The key to flowing in God's serving grace is not to be concerned with labels. What is important is that you serve from a heart of love.

Grace Gifts in Corinthians

Now concerning spiritual gifts, brethren, I do not want you to be ignorant.

1 Corinthians 12:1

In 1 Corinthians 12, the word translated "gifts" is also used in verses 4, 9, 28, 30, and 31, and it is the Greek word *charismata*. The root word is *charis*, the Greek word for grace, which we studied in Chapter 4. One noted Greek scholar said, "The charis of God manifests itself in various charismata."[5] In other words, the grace that God has place within us will be activated by the Holy Spirit to manifest as one of the gifts.

But one and the same Spirit works all these things, distributing to each one individually as He wills.

1 Corinthians 12:11

Paul lists nine manifestations or expressions of the Spirit in 1 Corinthians 12:8-10, which include the word of wisdom, the word of knowledge, faith, gifts of healings, the working of miracles, prophecy, discerning of spirits, different kinds of tongues, and the interpretation of tongues. Later in verse 28, Paul provides a somewhat overlapping list of other grace gifts and offices that benefit the Church: apostles, prophets, teachers, miracles, gifts of healings, helps, administrations, and varieties of tongues. He mentions interpretation of tongues again in verse 30.

It stands to reason that gifts flowing from the grace of God should be administered graciously. If you encounter a brother or sister who insists they have a gift but are being much less than gracious, such as trying to force their gift on others, demanding recognition for their gift or drawing attention to themselves as they operate in that gift, you can be assured something is amiss. It does not necessarily mean they have not received something from God, but they may have much maturing to do. Again,

I believe this is why Paul placed 1 Corinthians 13 (the great chapter on love) between chapters 12 and 14, the two most definitive chapters on manifestations of the Holy Spirit. Charismata (gifts of grace) should manifest and express the charis (grace) of God, not our carnality.

One commentary offers a great insight as to how spiritual gifts are to function in the church:

> Spiritual gifts are tools to build with not toys to play with or weapons to fight with. In the church at Corinth, the believers were tearing down the ministry because they were abusing spiritual gifts. They were using their gifts as ends in themselves and not as a means toward the end of building up the church. They so emphasized their spiritual gifts that they lost their spiritual graces! They had the gifts of the Spirit but were lacking in the fruit of the spirit—love, joy, peace, etc. (Gal. 5:22–23).[6]

In Ephesians 4:7, Paul tells that church that every one of them were recipients of God's grace. In verse 8, he explains that when Jesus ascended, He "gave gifts to men." Three questions that come to mind are:

- What are the gifts Jesus gave?

- For what purpose did He give them?

- For how long did He give them?

Paul answers these questions in Ephesians 4:11-16 NLT:

Now these are the gifts Christ gave to the church: the apostles, the prophets, the evangelists, and the pastors and teachers. Their responsibility is to equip God's people to do his work and build up the church, the body of Christ. This will continue until we all come to such unity in our faith and knowledge of God's Son that we will be mature in the Lord, measuring up to the full and complete standard of Christ.

Then we will no longer be immature like children. We won't be tossed and blown about by every wind of new teaching. We will not be influenced when people try to trick us with lies so clever they sound like the truth. Instead, we will speak the truth in love, growing in every way more and more like Christ, who is the head of his body, the church. He makes the whole body fit together perfectly. As each part does its own special work, it helps the other parts grow, so that the whole body is healthy and growing and full of love.

There are two predominant themes repeated in all these passages of Scripture pertaining to charismata, grace gifts or manifestations:

1. God's serving grace is the source of all gifts and manifestations that come from Him. He assigns them, so we cannot simply decide, "I want to be an apostle," or "I want to be a pastor." The Caller establishes our calling, and it behooves us to allow Him to show us what our assignments and gifts are. He knows what is best! As we trust Him in this, we can serve Him gladly, drawing continually on His grace, whether we are serving behind the pulpit or behind the scenes.

2. God has gifts and callings for every one of His children. Each one of us has a vital role to play, and He gave us His divine grace to empower and inspire us to do our part effectively and for His glory.

Please don't think if you are not a powerful preacher or dynamically gifted singer that God cannot use you! He is not looking to make celebrities; He wants to use servants. Dwight L. Moody said, "If this world is going to be reached, I am convinced that it must be done by men and women of average talent."[7] Don't get caught up comparing yourself with others, which can only lead to pride or inferiority, but be thankful for the gifts and callings God has given you to serve Him and His people.

Most people know George Washington Carver as the man who discovered hundreds of usages for peanuts, soy beans, and sweet potatoes. Many do not know that he was a man of prayer, who gave God glory for all the wisdom he had and the discoveries he made. Carver also spoke of the role of believers in the Church:

> There is going to be a great spiritual awakening in the world, and it is going to come from… plain, simple people who know—not simply believe—but actually know that God answers prayer. It is going to be a great revival of Christianity, not a revival of religion. This is going to be a revival of true Christianity. It is going to rise from the laymen, from men who are going about their work and putting God into what they do, from men who believe in prayer, and who want to make God real to mankind.[8]

Let's awaken to the fact that God wants to use every one of us and be fervent and diligent to be true servants of the Lord as we respond and yield to the grace and gifts He has placed in our lives.

Questions for Reflection and Discussion:

- What was new and fresh to you?
- What reinforced the understanding you already had?
- What challenged your previous or current understanding?
- Regarding sanctifying grace, explain the difference between the positional truth of who you are in Christ and the behavioral application of your spiritual walk or lifestyle.
- What would you say to a Christian who believed God's grace made their lifestyle irrelevant?
- How does God's sanctifying grace lead us into a life of obedience and holiness?
- How has knowing about sanctifying grace affected your personal idea of godly living? Personal discipline?
- Do you trust God for strengthening grace more during times of crisis and difficulty, or have you established a daily discipline of depending on God's strength for everything?
- How would what you know about God's strengthening grace affect what you would share with a person who believed that trusting God meant never facing any problems or challenges?
- After reading about sharing grace, how would you address the idea that God only cares about the spiritual needs of people?
- Explain the biblical relationship between grace and work in light of sharing grace.
- If tithing began as an act of consecration and faith by Abram, before the Law of Moses, what does that mean to you today?
- If sharing grace causes us to see giving not as a grievous burden but a joyous blessing, how much work has God done in your heart?
- It is clear from Scripture that Paul received serving grace to carry out his ministry, so how much was Paul and his own personal effort involved?
- When a person receives serving grace, does that mean you can serve effectively in any ministry office at any time? Would your gifts and calling prohibit you from fulfilling basic Christian responsibilities?

Part Five

How Do I Grow in God's Grace?

Chapter 17

THE JOY OF MORE GRACE

How sweet the name of Jesus sounds...my never-failing treasury, filled with boundless stores of grace!

—John Newton

Upon hearing the wonders of God's grace, you might ask, "Is it possible for me to experience more grace than I am right now?" You know the definition of grace is a free gift you can do nothing to earn or deserve, but you may have noticed that some Christians seem to have a greater awareness and understanding of grace. Perhaps it will help our understanding if we realize this truth: Grace is freely given, but it is not automatically enjoyed. Maybe the better question is, "How can I make sure that I'm walking in the awareness of God's grace, accessing and benefitting from it, and growing in it?"

Grace Is Not a Thing

And of His fullness we have all received, and grace for grace. For the law was given through Moses, but grace and truth came through Jesus Christ.

John 1:16-17

When you receive Jesus, you receive grace. It is important to understand that grace is not something that is received separate from Him. Sinclair B. Ferguson wisely said, "Grace is not a 'thing.' It is not a substance that can be measured or a commodity to be distributed. It is 'the grace of the Lord Jesus Christ' (2 Corinthians 13:14). In essence, it is Jesus Himself."[1] In another writing Ferguson also shared,

> There is a center to the Bible and its message of grace. It is found in Jesus Christ crucified and resurrected. Grace, therefore, must be preached in a way that is centered and focused on Jesus Christ Himself. We must never offer the benefits of the gospel without the Benefactor Himself.[2]

The Amplified Bible translates John 1:16, "For out of His fullness (abundance) we have all received [all had a share and we were all supplied with] one grace after another and spiritual blessing upon spiritual blessing and even favor upon favor and gift [heaped] upon gift."

It appears Jesus brings many expressions and experiences of grace into our lives. *The New Bible Commentary* says, "The fullness does not come to us all at once but in a progression of gracious experiences."[3] Another commentary says, "Here the picture is 'grace' taking the place of 'grace' like the manna fresh each morning, new grace for the new day and the new service."[4]

Colossians 2:10 NLT says that you are "complete through your union with Christ," and yet God's grace comes to us in wave after glorious wave throughout our walk with Him. We can understand this by considering marriage. When a man and woman are pronounced husband and wife, they are legally married. As they grow through the years and work through life's challenges together, they get to know each other more and more, and they have additional opportunities to support and show kindness, patience, and understanding to one another. Some couples are legally married, but instead of being good to one another, walls of offense, unforgiveness, and bitterness are built. These walls keep them from enjoying the wonderful relationship God intended. They still are legally married, but the warmth, camaraderie, and sweet fellowship they could have had is non-existent.

Likewise, "The One who joins himself with the Lord becomes one spirit with him" (1 Corinthians 6:17 we). Our union with Jesus begins the moment we are born again, but the quality our fellowship with Him can vary significantly depending on how we interact with Him. He offers us more grace for every situation and literally urges us to draw upon His love, empowerment, and ability as we encounter new phases of life. But we have to receive it.

Five Ways to Receive More Grace

We never earn grace, but if we respond in a right way we can enjoy more grace and partake of it, especially during times of need. Following are five of these responses.

1. Faith

Therefore, having been justified by faith, we have peace with God through our Lord Jesus Christ, through whom also **we have access by faith into this grace in which we stand,** *and rejoice in hope of the glory of God.*

Romans 5:1-2 (bold mine)

For by grace you have been saved **through faith,** *and that not of yourselves; it is the gift of God.*

Ephesians 2:8 (bold mine)

It has been said that grace is God's hand extended to us, and faith is our trusting hand put into His. His grace offers us Himself and His blessings, while our faith accepts, receives, and lays hold of what He is freely offering.

- Grace is Jesus saying, "I provide."

- Faith is us saying, "I receive."

- Grace says, "Because I love you, I have provided for you."

- Faith says, "Because You love me, I believe and receive Your provision."

Grace and faith are never contradictory or in opposition to one another; rather, they are inseparably interdependent upon each other and work seamlessly together. If God did not provide blessings by His grace, we could believe until we were blue in the face, but nothing would happen. Likewise, grace requires faith for God's blessings to be received. God is a gentleman, and He will not force His blessings upon us.

Growing in grace is about relationship and intimacy with God. Faith is our part—our response, but even our faith originated with God's grace. That is why Paul, speaking of grace and faith, went on to say, "...and that not of yourselves; it is the gift of God." The very faith through which we are saved came from God (Romans 10:17)!

Jerome, an early church father who died in 420 A.D., addressed this very issue when commenting on Ephesians 2:8:

> Paul says this in case the secret thought should steal upon us that "if we are not saved by our own works, at least we are saved by our own faith, and so in another way our salvation is of ourselves." Thus he added the statement that faith too is not in our own will but in God's gift. Not that he means to take away free choice from humanity...but that even this very freedom of choice has God as its author, and all things are to be referred to his generosity, in that he has even allowed us to will the good.[5]

A Christian has no business boasting about anything, including his faith. (See also John 3:27; 1 Corinthians 1:27-31 and 4:7.)

For I say, through the grace given to me, to everyone who is among you, not to think of himself more highly than he ought to think, but to think soberly, as God has dealt to each one a measure of faith.

Romans 12:3

God gave us "a measure of faith" through which we embrace His grace, first in salvation and then throughout our Christian lives. Our faith continues to partake of grace as we meet every challenge of life.

Therefore, having been justified by faith, we have peace with God through our Lord Jesus Christ, through whom also we have access by faith into this grace in which we stand.

Romans 5:1-2

You have access to God's grace through your faith in Him. Like opening a door gives you access to a room, exercising your faith in God gives you access to His grace. We need both faith and grace to enjoy God's blessings. Grace is God granting the provision while faith enables man to access the provision.

2. The Knowledge of God

Grace and peace be multiplied to you in the knowledge of God and of Jesus our Lord.

2 Peter 1:2

Here is another verse that tells us we can grow in grace, and this time the Word reveals we do so through knowing God and the Lord Jesus Christ. The Greek word for "knowledge" means full knowledge. This implies more than knowing about God, accumulating facts or having information about Him; it refers to knowing God in a personal and intimate way—a heart experience.

Knowledge—the true knowledge of God—is tremendously important in our Christian lives. In Hosea 4:6, God said, "My people are destroyed for lack of knowledge." Jesus said, "If you abide in My word, you are My disciples indeed. And you shall know the truth, and the truth shall make you free" (John 8:31-32). The apostle Paul said:

> *I also count all things loss for the excellence of the knowledge of Christ Jesus my Lord, for whom I have suffered the loss of all things, and count them as rubbish, that I may gain Christ...that I may know Him and the power of His resurrection, and the fellowship of His sufferings.*
>
> Philippians 3:8,10

For Paul, knowing Jesus was the great quest of His heart, and though we would surely consider Paul to have an amazing relationship with the Lord, he was mindful that there was always more to know of Him. He said, "Now I know in part, but then I shall know just as I also am known" (1 Corinthians 13:12). He also prayed for all believers to know God intimately:

> *I pray that from his glorious, unlimited resources he will empower you with inner strength through his Spirit. Then Christ will make his home in your hearts as you trust in him. Your roots will grow down into God's love and keep you strong. And may you have the power to understand, as all God's people should, how wide, how long, how high, and how deep his love is. May you experience the love of Christ, though it is too great to understand fully. Then you will be made complete with all the fullness of life and power that comes from God.*
>
> Ephesians 3:16-19 NLT

How do you know God and thereby grow in His grace? We saw earlier that grace initially came to us in the Person of Jesus Christ, and today, God continues to reveal Himself and to impart His grace to us through His Word and the Holy Spirit. The message we preach is called the gospel of the grace of God and the word of his grace (Acts 20:24,32). The Holy Spirit is called the Spirit of grace (Hebrews 10:29). Whenever we get into God's Word and spend time in His presence, we are partaking of grace. This applies in a corporate setting (receiving the Word as it is taught and worshipping corporately) as well as spending time one-on-one with God in the Word and worship. Ephesians 4:29 even tells us that we can impart grace to one another through godly, edifying words. All of this helps you know Him, and the more you know Him, the more you will enjoy and benefit from His grace.

3. Humility

But He gives more grace. Therefore He says:

> *"God resists the proud,*
> *But gives grace to the humble."*

Therefore submit to God. Resist the devil and he will flee from you. Draw near to God and He will draw near to you.

James 4:6-8

Yes, all of you be submissive to one another, and be clothed with humility, for

> *"God resists the proud,*
> *But gives grace to the humble."*

Therefore humble yourselves under the mighty hand of God, that He may exalt you in due time.

1 Peter 5:5-6

Some may believe that God never resists anyone, but the Apostles James and Peter made it clear that He does. While God gives grace (and more grace) to the humble—to the person who depends and relies upon Him, He resists the proud individual who arrogantly believes He can do it on his own without God's help. The prideful man says, "God, I don't need you. I can do it all by myself."

I will tell you how serious this is. When James said God resists the proud, the word he used for "resists" is a Greek military term that means "to battle against."[7] God wants nothing more than to bless you, but when you are proud, arrogant, and independent, you have declared war on Him! God is not out to destroy you when you get puffed up in pride or deceived into arrogance, but He cannot bless or encourage your proud, self-destructive attitude or behavior. It is sin, and He must oppose it.

Dwight L. Moody said, "God sends no one away empty except those who are full of themselves."[8] Thomas à Kempis asked, "What good is it for you to be able to discuss the Trinity with great profundity, if you lack humility, and thereby offend the Trinity?"[9] The moment we think or say, "Okay God, I can take it from here," we have ceased to recognize our absolute need for Him.

You must remain aware of your need for God's presence and sustaining grace. As long you acknowledge your need for Him, you will continue to enjoy, experience, and benefit from His grace growing inside you.

4. Boldness

It may seem a bit unusual that boldness would be in the same list as humility, but the two are perfectly compatible. Arrogance is the opposite of humility and actually a perversion of boldness. Arrogance is pride based on self; boldness is confidence based on God.

> *So then, since we have a great High Priest who has entered Heaven, Jesus the Son of God, let us hold firmly to what we believe. This High Priest of ours understands our weaknesses, for he faced all of the same testings we do, yet he did not sin. So let us come boldly to the throne of our gracious God. There we will receive his mercy, and we will find grace to help us when we need it most.*
>
> Hebrews 4:14-16 NLT

What an amazing invitation from God! We are invited to come boldly before His throne—and thank God His is a throne of grace not judgment! What will we find there? Criticism? Fault-finding? Condemnation? No! He said we would receive mercy and find His grace when we need it most.

All of us face challenges in life that will make us realize our complete dependency upon God. During those times, He invites you to partake of, draw from, experience, and enjoy the mercy and grace He has for you. Proverbs 28:1 says, "The righteous are bold as a lion." When you know God has cleansed you from all sin and has made you His child, and is one hundred percent for you, that sparks boldness in your heart!

In Acts 4, Peter and John were called on the carpet by the religious leaders for preaching Jesus to the people. These were the same leaders who had been involved in the crucifixion of Jesus, so this was a very dangerous situation for the two disciples. Instead of backing down, however, Peter gave a powerful testimony of Jesus as the Savior of the world. His remarks concluded with, "There is salvation in no one else! God has given no other name under heaven by which we must be saved" (Acts 4:12 NLT).

How did the religious leaders react?

The members of the council were amazed when they saw the boldness of Peter and John, for they could see that they were ordinary men with no special training in the Scriptures. They also recognized them as men who had been with Jesus.

Acts 4:13 NLT

Peter and John were threatened again and told not to preach the gospel; but then they were released. When they joined their fellow believers, what did they do? They prayed. It was a time of danger, and they went boldly before God's throne (you can read their prayer in Acts 4:23-30). The following verses show how they were living out the principle of Hebrews 4:16:

And when they had prayed, the place where they were assembled to-gether was shaken; and they were all filled with the Holy Spirit, and they spoke the Word of God with **boldness.**

And with **great power** *the apostles gave witness to the resurrection of the Lord Jesus. And* **great grace** *was upon them all.*

Acts 4:31,33 (bold mine)

What about you? Is there a threatening situation you are facing, a great challenge or trial that has come against you? The same throne of grace the early Christians accessed is open to you now, and you have been invited to come boldly before God there.

You may say, "But I don't feel bold. This is really serious." Boldness is not based on how you feel; it is based solely on the character of God, and you can trust Him to give you the wisdom and strength you need to prevail and be "more than a conqueror" in your situation.

5. Undying Love

In the beginning of this book, we saw the blend of love and grace. Because God loves us, He gives us His grace to be saved and to live joyfully and successfully. Ephesians 6:24 highlights this connection:

- "Grace be with all those who love our Lord Jesus Christ in sincerity. Amen" (NKJV).

- "Grace be with all those who love our Lord Jesus Christ with incorruptible love" (NASBU).

First John 4:10 and 19 say, "This is love, not that we loved God, but that He loved us," and, "We love Him because He first loved us." Our ability to love God came from Him. God's wonderful love and grace were imparted to us when we were born again, and John indicates that the grace we walk in grows as we love Jesus in sincerity, without corruption, and with an undying love.

Let me encourage you to pray this prayer and to saturate your being with it, so the words of these truths flow freely from your heart on a regular basis.

"Dear Heavenly Father, I thank You that through Your Son Jesus I have received wave upon wave of Your wonderful grace. I receive your grace by faith, and I thank You that Your grace is multiplied unto me through knowing You for who You really are. I recognize that I can do nothing without You, and I know that as I humble myself before You, I thank You that You give me even more grace. I thank You that I don't have to feel inferior or unworthy before You, and that You have invited me to come boldly before Your throne of grace to obtain mercy and to find grace to help me in my times of need. I also thank You that Your love has been shed abroad in my heart, and You give me grace as I love You with an undying, incorruptible, and sincere love. I want to be like Jesus, who was full of grace, who had grace resting upon Him, and from His lips flowed gracious words. Thank You that I am the grace child of a gracious God. In Jesus' name I pray, amen."

Chapter 18

DON'T SHORT-CIRCUIT GRACE!

I f it is possible to reduce and diminish grace in our lives, we need to know how to "plug that leak." This is not just a theological discussion; it is extremely practical! We need God's grace to become more like Christ Jesus and to fulfill our God-given destiny. Bible history is full of accounts of God extending His grace to individuals and nations then being rejected. Others only received and walked in a fraction of the grace and blessing He desired to give them.

> *"For it was I, the LORD your God,*
>> *who rescued you from the land of Egypt.*
>> *Open your mouth wide, and I will fill it with good things.*
> *"But no, my people wouldn't listen.*
>> *Israel did not want me around.*
> *So I let them follow their own stubborn desires,*
>> *living according to their own ideas.*
> *Oh, that my people would listen to me!*
>> *Oh, that Israel would follow me, walking in my paths!*
> *How quickly I would then subdue their enemies!*
>> *How soon my hands would be upon their foes!*
> *Those who hate the LORD would cringe before him;*
>> *they would be doomed forever*

But I would feed you with the finest wheat.
I would satisfy you with wild honey from the rock.

Psalm 81:10-16 NLT

Jonah 2:8 (NIV) says that those who cling to worthless idols forfeit the grace that could be theirs. The idea of "forfeiting grace" reminds me of the lyrics in the old song, "What a Friend We Have in Jesus":

> O what peace we often forfeit,
> O what needless pain we bear,
> All because we do not carry,
> Everything to God in prayer.

Can we really forfeit God's peace and experience needless pain? Many scriptures support this, and life has enough challenges and difficulties, that I don't care to experience pain needlessly.

Jesus was grieved that the City of Jerusalem refused the saving grace of God He brought them. In Luke 13:34 NLT, He said, "O Jerusalem, Jerusalem, the city that kills the prophets and stones God's messengers! How often I have wanted to gather your children together as a hen protects her chicks beneath her wings, but you wouldn't let me." The depth of Jesus' compassion toward the Jewish people is further revealed in Luke 19:41, "He saw the city and wept over it."

Those words paint quite a picture. "I have wanted to... but you wouldn't let me." Jesus' desire to see them receive His Father's saving grace was not based on their flawless performance or perfection. Even though He said they had killed the prophets and stoned God's messengers, He was still reaching out to them! This is what grace is about: God is for us even when we are against Him. As Romans 5:8 says, "God demonstrates His own love toward us, in that while we were still sinners, Christ died for us."

New Testament Believers

You might say, "Well that was the Old Testament and before Jesus went to the Cross. They didn't understand grace. I'm born again and have received His grace." If you received God's saving grace, you can still short-circuit other expressions of His grace in your Christian life. Are there certain areas of your life where you may be stopping the flow of His grace—sanctifying, strengthening, sharing, or serving? After all, the benefits of God's grace are not automatically applied, experienced, and enjoyed simply because we are His children. For example, 2 Corinthians 6:1 says, "We...plead with you not to receive the grace of God in vain."

- "We beg you not to accept this marvelous gift of God's kindness and then ignore it" (NLT).

- "Do not receive it to no purpose" (AMP).

- "Do not let the grace that you received from God be for nothing" (NCV).

- "We beg you, please don't squander one bit of this marvelous life God has given us" (MSG).

My old self has been crucified with Christ. It is no longer I who live, but Christ lives in me. So I live in this earthly body by trusting in the Son of God, who loved me and gave himself for me. **I do not treat the grace of God as meaningless.** *For if keeping the law could make us right with God, then there was no need for Christ to die.*

Galatians 2:20-21 NLT

The King James Version renders verse 21, "I do not frustrate the grace of God," while the Amplified Bible says, "[Therefore, I do not treat God's gracious gift as something of minor importance and defeat its very purpose]; I do not set aside and invalidate and frustrate and nullify the grace (unmerited favor) of God."

According to these scriptures, New Testament believers can refuse, ignore, not use, waste, squander, mistreat, frustrate, minimize, defeat, set aside, invalidate, and nullify the grace of God. So we must be diligent to do the opposite! We must commit ourselves to always accept, highly regard, utilize to the fullest, encourage, covet, maximize, focus on, and build our lives upon God's grace. We must live from the essence of who we are in Christ Jesus and from the grace that He has poured freely into our lives.

Falling From Grace

You have become estranged from Christ, you who attempt to be justified by law; you have fallen from grace.

Galatians 5:4

What does it mean to fall from grace? Was Paul saying the Galatians had lost their salvation and were no longer children of God? Unfortunately, many believers have reached this terrible conclusion and, as a result, live in fear that they are lost. However, does the internal evidence within this epistle support that opinion? Consider that nine times Paul refers to the recipients of his letter as brethren. He also refers to them as children in reference to their relationship to God.

- "My little children, for whom I labor in birth again until Christ is formed in you..." (Galatians 4:19).

- "Now we, brethren, as Isaac was, are children of promise" (Galatians 4:28).

- "So then, brethren, we are not children of the bondwoman but of the free" (Galatians 4:31).

In addition to referring to the Galatians as brothers and as children of God, Paul further refers to them as "sons of God."

- "For you are all sons of God through faith in Christ Jesus" (Galatians 3:26).

- "And because you are sons, God has sent forth the Spirit of His Son into your hearts, crying out, 'Abba, Father!'" (Galatians 4:6).

Paul still considered the Galatians to be children of God, but he was deeply concerned and alarmed that a gross distortion of the gospel was leading them away from the liberty and richness of faith in Christ alone. False teachers had come in and had told the Galatian believers that faith in Christ was not enough; they needed to be circumcised and begin keeping the Law in addition to trusting in Him.

Paul was distressed that they had been deceived by these lies and were going backward in their spiritual walk. He pointed out that justification by keeping the Law and justification by grace through faith are mutually exclusive, and he contended that a Christian life not based on grace is oxymoronic. He argued vehemently against the deceptive detour they had taken and referred to it as a perversion of the gospel (Galatians 1:7), declaring they were foolish and had been bewitched to embrace such false doctrine (Galatians 3:1,3).

While Paul was deeply disturbed about the bondage to which the Galatians had reverted, his harshest words were not against the victims of the legalistic teaching but its proponents. He said, "But even if we, or an angel from heaven, preach any other gospel to you than what we have preached to you, let him be accursed" (Galatians 1:8), and "I just wish that those troublemakers who want to mutilate you by circumcision would mutilate themselves" (Galatians 5:12 NLT). The tone of his entire letter reveals how seriously he took this issue, and how much he valued believers continuing to walk in grace for the remainder of their spiritual journey, not frustrating or falling from the influence of God's grace over time.

The Spirit of Grace

In the New Testament we find a statement about unbelievers who resist the Holy Spirit (Acts 7:51), and we find admonitions for believers not to quench or grieve the Holy Spirit (1 Thessalonians 5:19; Ephesians 4:30). As believers, we may have missed it in these areas on occasion, and forgiveness is available, but we desire to develop our awareness, sensitivity, and obedience to the Lord so that in the future we live lives that are yielded to the leading and the influence of the Holy Spirit.

There is an even more stern and sober warning found in the book of Hebrews that pertains to insulting the Spirit of grace:

> *For if we sin willfully after we have received the knowledge of the truth, there no longer remains a sacrifice for sins, but a certain fearful expectation of judgment, and fiery indignation which will devour the adversaries. Anyone who has rejected Moses' law dies without mercy on the testimony of two or three witnesses. Of how much worse punishment, do you suppose, will he be thought worthy who has trampled the Son of God underfoot, counted the blood of the covenant by which he was sanctified a common thing, and insulted the Spirit of grace?*
>
> Hebrews 10:26-29

What, exactly, does it mean to insult the Spirit of grace? Some believers, especially those who are highly conscientious, find this very troubling. I have had people approach me over the years in torment, fearing they had committed the unpardonable sin, had insulted the "Spirit of grace," and were now going to be lost forever. Their rationale was that they were tempted, they knew it was wrong, and they did it anyway. Now they feel they are beyond the reach of God's grace and forgiveness.

I think it is important to look at all of this in context. Did they sin in some area? Yes. But do they meet all of those qualifications that are mentioned in Hebrews? I seriously doubt it. I've asked individuals who were distressed in this way, "If Jesus were to come in here right now, would you trample Him underfoot?"

"No! I would bow down and worship Him and ask Him to forgive me."

"If the Lord told you that His blood had been shed for your forgiveness, would you consider His blood a common thing?"

"Oh, no, there is nothing more precious than the blood of Jesus."

"And if the Holy Spirit spoke to you right now and told you He was here to apply God's grace and forgiveness to your life, would you reject Him and insult Him?"

"Never! I would welcome Him and thank Him for bringing God's grace to comfort to me."

Such individuals may have sinned, but they certainly have not lost their salvation. They need to accept God's forgiveness according to 1 John 1:9. Just a few verses later, Hebrews 10:39 NLT says, "But we are not like those who turn away from God to their own destruction. We are the faithful ones, whose souls will be saved." We need to focus on scriptures that provide assurance of our salvation and facilitate the growth and flow of the grace of God in our lives. The devil will try to torment our minds, telling us we have lost our salvation and are no longer God's child. We must meditate on God's Word and grow in grace instead.

Some verses that are especially reassuring include:

- "All that the Father gives Me will come to Me, and the one who comes to Me I will by no means cast out" (John 6:37).

- "My sheep hear My voice, and I know them, and they follow Me. And I give them eternal life, and they shall never perish; neither shall anyone snatch them out of My hand. My Father, who has given them to Me, is greater than all; and no one is able to snatch them out of My Father's hand" (John 10:27-29).

- "For I am persuaded that neither death nor life, nor angels nor principalities nor powers, nor things present nor things to come, nor height nor depth, nor any other created thing, shall be able to separate us from the love of God which is in Christ Jesus our Lord" (Romans 8:38-39).

We need to know and abide in God's love so that we are not insecure about losing our salvation every time we sin or make a mistake. Shun sin? Absolutely, but never forget that the words of the old hymn are true: "Grace, grace, God's grace, Grace that will pardon and cleanse within; Grace, grace, God's grace, Grace that is greater than all our sin."

Don't Be Deceived

Hebrews 3:13 NLT says, "You must warn each other every day, while it is still 'today,' so that none of you will be deceived by sin and hardened against God." Even though sin may be forgiven, if a person persists in sin, it brings deception and hardness toward God into their life.

In Revelation 2:21 NLT, Jesus spoke of a so-called prophetess. He said, "I gave her time to repent, but she does not want to turn away from her immorality." First Timothy 4:1-2 speaks of those who will depart from "the faith" and sear their consciences. In other words, they will become completely insensitive to sin and it won't bother them anymore. Part of the deception of sin is that when negative consequences don't occur immediately, the person thinks, *I can sin and get away with it; nothing bad is going to happen.* Some may even think that God is fine with their behavior since no consequences are immediately experienced, but the reason no consequences are happening is because the Holy Spirit is giving them time to repent! If they continue sinning, eventually they don't even feel guilty anymore—but there will come a time when they will reap what they have sown.

> *Do not be deceived, God is not mocked; for whatever a man sows, that he will also reap. For he who sows to his flesh will of the flesh reap corruption, but he who sows to the Spirit will of the Spirit reap everlasting life.*
>
> Galatians 6:7-8

A prime example of the deception of sin involves pornography. Surveys have found an alarming incidence of this among Christian men. When they seek help and break free of this bondage, their testimonies are typically quite similar. They started viewing pornography, perhaps what is called 'soft' porn casually, but after a while they became de-sensitized to it and did not receive the same high or sense of intoxication. Therefore, they sought more intense and deviant forms. Before they realized it, they were addicted. They never thought they would sink that low, but "they were hardened through the deceitfulness of sin" (Hebrews 3:13). This is a true saying: "Sin will take you farther than you want to go, keep you longer than you want to stay, and cost you more than you want to pay."

This does not mean that God quit loving them, or that He has rejected them eternally, but He is waiting for them to reach out to Him to receive forgiveness, cleansing, and restoration. They need to be restored to purity and receive healing for any damage that occurred in relationships or other areas of their lives as a result of their sinful behavior. God is waiting for them to respond to His sanctifying grace.

If you play with fire, you are going to get burned! Instead of yielding to temptation, allow God's grace to empower you and keep you on the right path. If you have already missed it, allow His grace to pull you out of the ditch and give you a new start.

Therefore strengthen the hands which hang down, and the feeble knees,
and make straight paths for your feet, so that what is lame may not be
dislocated, but rather be healed.

Hebrews 12:12-13

"But how do I do this?" you might ask. "I have fought this area of sin, this horrible habit, for so long!" There are some situations where you will achieve victory simply by yielding to God's Spirit and getting your mind renewed by the Word of God. In other, more deeply-rooted situations, there can be tremendous benefit by establishing meaningful boundaries and becoming part of an accountability group.

There are Bible-based groups that provide a loving, grace-governed atmosphere and help people in recovery. In these, believers find help by honestly confessing their faults to one another and exhorting and encouraging one another (James 5:16 and Hebrews 3:13).

Don't Fall Short!

For consider Him who endured such hostility from sinners against
Himself, lest you become weary and discouraged in your souls. You have
not yet resisted to bloodshed, striving against sin. And you have forgot-
ten the exhortation which speaks to you as to sons:

"My son, do not despise the chastening of the Lord,
Nor be discouraged when you are rebuked by Him;
For whom the Lord loves He chastens,
And scourges every son whom He receives."

If you endure chastening, God deals with you as with sons; for what son
is there whom a father does not chasten? But if you are without chas-
tening, of which all have become partakers, then you are illegitimate
and not sons. Furthermore, we have had human fathers who corrected

us, and we paid them respect. Shall we not much more readily be in
subjection to the Father of spirits and live? For they indeed for a few
days chastened us as seemed best to them, but He for our profit, that we
may be partakers of His holiness. Now no chastening seems to be joyful
for the present, but painful; nevertheless, afterward it yields the peace-
able fruit of righteousness to those who have been trained by it.

Pursue peace with all people, and holiness, without which no one will
see the Lord: looking carefully lest anyone fall short of the grace of God;
lest any root of bitterness springing up cause trouble, and by this many
become defiled.

Hebrews 12:3-11,14-15

This passage of Scripture addresses how we overcome in life, receive correction from God, and partake of His holiness. There is a work of God in our hearts to keep us from becoming offended when we are faced with three specific challenges: the hostility of sinners or unbelievers (verse 3), our personal battle against sin (verse 4), and the discipline of the Lord (verses 5-11). We need God's grace to respond appropriately in each case.

Hebrews 12:15 in the NLT says, "Look after each other so that none of you fails to receive the grace of God. Watch out that no poisonous root of bitterness grows up to trouble you, corrupting many." It seems that believers can help each other greatly to continue walking in God's grace. If we don't cling to grace then we will become bitter; and such bitterness can bring trouble and defilement into many other lives.

Whether we struggle with persecution for the gospel's sake, a temptation to sin, or submitting to the Lord's correction, we can respond rightly or wrongly. We can respond by drawing upon God's wonderful grace and allowing Him to fill us with His power, love, and humility, or we can become poisoned with bitterness, refusing to forgive and love as He has forgiven and loved us. By yielding to God's grace, we will not fall short.

When God chastens us, He is not abusing us; rather, He is training us as a parent would a child. The purpose of His discipline is not to harm us or beat us down, but to mature and develop us. Hebrews 12:10 tells us that He disciplines us "for our profit, that we may be partakers of His holiness," and in verse 11, His discipline enables us to produce, "the peaceable fruit of righteousness" in our lives. I think the first two verses of Hebrews 12 say it all:

> *Therefore we also, since we are surrounded by so great a cloud of witnesses, let us lay aside every weight, and the sin which so easily ensnares us, and let us run with endurance the race that is set before us, looking unto Jesus, the author and finisher of our faith, who for the joy that was set before Him endured the cross, despising the shame, and has sat down at the right hand of the throne of God.*
>
> Hebrews 12:1-2

We will not fall short of the grace of God in our Christian lives as long as we keep our eyes on Jesus, the author and finisher of our faith. Then we will partake of His grace with joy—and run our race with victorious endurance!

Dear Heavenly Father, I come to You in the name of Jesus, expressing my desire to always have Your wonderful grace flowing abundantly in every area of my life. With Your help, I know I will never forfeit the grace that You have for me. I pray and believe that today I will not receive Your grace in vain or ignore Your kindness toward me. The desire of my heart is to value and esteem Your grace highly, to never frustrate Your grace or treat it as meaningless. With Your help, I never want to fall away from or fall short of Your grace. I always desire to lean upon and lean into Your grace.

I also thank You that if I ever do fail to enjoy, benefit, or take full advantage of Your grace, You won't reject me or cast me out, but You will remind me I am Your child and son/daughter. With that in mind, I never want to be deceived by sin and hardened against You. I desire to grow in grace and in the knowledge—the personal knowledge—of who You are. In Jesus' name, amen.

Questions for Reflection and Discussion:

- What was new and fresh to you?

- What reinforced the understanding you already had?

- What challenged your previous or current understanding?

- What should be your response when you learn you can receive more grace, have grace multiplied in your life, and receive wave after wave of grace throughout your life?

- How do grace and faith work together?

- What does it mean to fall from grace? Quench the Spirit? Grieve the Spirit?

- What does it mean in Hebrews 3:13 NLT, where the Holy Spirit warns you not to be, "deceived by sin and hardened against God"?

Part Four

What's the Controversy About Grace?

Chapter 19

COMPLEMENTARY
ATTRIBUTES

Regarding the debate about faith and works: It's like asking
which blade in a pair of scissors is most important.

—C.S. Lewis[1]

In my note to you at the beginning of this book, I said I would address the problems I believed had arisen regarding the teaching
about grace. To understand how this error arises, we have to first
understand that grace does not stand alone. It was never God's inten-
tion for grace to be an independent spiritual force. Whether love, faith,
or grace, all of the expressions and attributes of God are complementary
and connect seamlessly to make us healthy, productive believers. If we
isolate grace (or any other doctrine) in an exclusionary way, it will become
skewed and out of proportion in our lives. We will fail to appreciate that
God has woven together all the aspects of His character and nature to
make us whole and fully effective as His children.

For example, years ago while studying the book of James, I saw that
four powerful spiritual principles were addressed in the first few verses
of the first chapter: joy, faith, patience, and wisdom. I realized I had seen
people try to be successful in their Christian lives by using faith, but many
times they had lost their joy, lacked endurance, or were not exercising

wisdom. I developed a message from those four points called "The Four-Wheel-Drive Christian."

In driving, you get far better traction when you have all four tires pulling, especially in adverse conditions. Likewise, we will do much better in our Christian lives if we are operating with a full arsenal of truth. This is why Paul placed great value upon proclaiming "the whole counsel of God" (Acts 20:27) and why he admonished believers to put on "the whole armor of God" (Ephesians 6:11). If you just emphasize one part of the Word and only put on one part of your spiritual armor, you will be off balance and vulnerable.

Imagine an anatomy class of future physicians, who are learning about various parts of the human body. The students can certainly focus their attention on one part, such as the heart, for awhile; however, when it comes to treating a person medically, a physician cannot examine the heart without considering its relationship to the rest of the body. The heart is dependent on the blood vessels, the lungs, and many other organs to work correctly. Moreover, the rest of the body is dependent on the heart. All the parts of the physical body must work together for us to be healthy and functioning.

Likewise, we can focus on grace for the purpose of study and discussion, but when it comes to living the Christian life, grace is one of many expressions of God in our lives that we must consider. I pray no one reads this book and says, "I used to live by faith, but now I live by grace." The truths of the Bible are not either-or propositions; they are all-inclusive considerations, and we must embrace all of God's truths.

No study on any biblical topic should build an altar around that particular truth and shut the door on the rest of biblical doctrine. No doctrine should be elevated inappropriately above any other. Jesus did not say we would live by isolated or selected words from God. He said in Luke 4:4, "It is written, 'Man shall not live by bread alone, but by every word that proceeds from the mouth of God.'"We are to live by every word that proceeds from the mouth of God.

All of the Above

I have called these attributes complementary because the truths and blessings that flow from the heart of God toward us are never contradictory or in competition with one another. He has placed them all in our lives, and that is why we must learn how to rightly divide the Word of God (2 Timothy 2:15). Then we can see each truth, each attribute of God in the harmonious, seamless blend He intended.

Justification, or being made and declared right with God, is a vitally important doctrine. It is very interesting to see the various angles from which Paul presents justification in the book of Romans:

- "...being justified freely by His grace" (Romans 3:24).
- "...was raised to secure our justification" (Romans 4:25 AMP).
- "Therefore, having been justified by faith,..." (Romans 5:1).
- "Having now been justified by His blood,..." (Romans 5:9).

We could read the above verses and wonder, "So how is it that we are justified? Is it by grace, the resurrection, faith, or the blood?" The correct answer is "All of the above." This is why we cannot exclusively focus on one biblical principle while ignoring and neglecting others. God could have chosen to communicate with us in a one-dimensional way, but He chose to give us a multi-dimensional perspective of His nature and His work. If we isolate one truth from other complementary truths or exalt one truth above all others, we will end up with a distorted perspective of God and His Word, as well as who we are and how we are to live as His children.

Grace and...

At the risk of sounding like an elementary school report card, we might say that grace "plays well with others." Grace does not invalidate or make obsolete any other New Testament truth. Grace honors and works in conjunction with every other attribute and expression of God in our lives. Consider all the ways the Bible presents God's grace as it collaborates and harmonizes with other spiritual forces:

- Grace and Speech (Psalm 45:2; Proverbs 22:11; Luke 4:22; Ephesians 4:29; Colossians 4:6)

- Grace and Glory (Psalm 84:11; Proverbs 4:9; John 1:14)

- Grace and Humility (Proverbs 3:34; James 4:6; 1 Peter 5:5)

- Grace and Supplication (Zechariah 12:10)

- Strength, Wisdom, and Grace (Luke 2:40)

- Grace and Truth (John 1:14,17)

- Power and Grace (Acts 4:33)

- Grace and Churches (Acts 11:23; 2 Corinthians 8:1, Revelation 1:4)

- Boldness, Grace, Signs, and Wonders (Acts 14:3)

- Grace and Commissioning (Acts 14:26)

- Grace and Salvation (Acts 15:11; Ephesians 2:5,8; Titus 2:11)

- Grace and the Gospel (Acts 20:24)

- Grace, Edification, Inheritance, and Sanctification (Acts 20:32)

- Grace and Apostleship (Romans 1:5)

- Justification, Grace, and Redemption (Romans 3:24)

- Grace and Faith (Romans 4:16; 5:2; Ephesians 2:8)

- Grace and Rejoicing in Hope (Romans 5:2)

- Grace and the Gift (Romans 5:15; Ephesians 2:8)

- Grace and Righteousness (Romans 5:17,21; Galatians 2:21)

- Grace and Eternal Life (Romans 5:21)

- Grace and a Discontinuation from Sin (Romans 6:1-2,15)

- Gifts and Grace (Romans 12:6)

- Grace and Building (1 Corinthians 3:10)

- Grace and Enablement (1 Corinthians 15:10; Ephesians 3:7)

- Grace and Labor (1 Corinthians 15:10)

- Simplicity, Sincerity, and Grace (2 Corinthians 1:12)

- Grace and Thanksgiving (2 Corinthians 4:15)

- Grace and Sacrifice (2 Corinthians 8:9; Hebrews 2:9)

- Grace, Sufficiency, and Abundance (2 Corinthians 9:8)

- Grace, Strength, and Power (2 Corinthians 12:9)

- Grace, Separation, and Calling (Galatians 1:15)

- Grace and Acceptance (Ephesians 1:6)

- Redemption, Forgiveness, Grace (Ephesians 1:7)

- Grace and Kindness (Ephesians 2:7)

- Grace and Preaching (Ephesians 3:8)

- Grace and Partnership (Philippians 1:7)

- Grace and Singing (Colossians 3:16)

- Grace and Glorification (2 Thessalonians 1:12)

- Consolation, Hope, and Grace (2 Thessalonians 2:16)

- Grace, Mercy, and Peace (1 Timothy 1:2; 2 Timothy 1:2, Titus 1:4)

- Grace, Faith, and Love (1 Timothy 1:14)

- Grace, Purpose, and Calling (2 Timothy 1:9)

- Grace and Strength (2 Timothy 2:1)

- Grace and Rejection of Ungodliness and Worldly Lusts (Titus 2:12)

- Grace and Sober, Righteous, and Godly Living (Titus 2:12)

- Grace and Justification (Titus 3:7)

- Boldness, Grace, and Mercy (Hebrews 4:16)

- Grace and the Blood of the Covenant (Hebrews 10:29)

- Grace, Service, Reverence, and Godly Fear (Hebrews 12:28)

- Grace and Peace (1 Peter 1:2; 2 Peter 1:2; Revelation 1:4)

- Marriage, Grace, and Prayer (1 Peter 3:7)

- Service, Stewardship, and Grace (1 Peter 4:10)

- Grace and Knowledge (2 Peter 3:18)

If you really want to be blessed, look up and read the verses listed above. Examine the working relationship between grace and the other spiritual parts of your life. You will see there is no competition between them. They are not striving against one another, vying for your attention above all others. They work together to maintain your spiritual health.

You will also notice that in some of these verses, grace is the root and the other attribute(s) or truth(s) listed are the fruit. For example, "Grace and Sober, Righteous, and Godly Living" or "Grace and Singing." Grace provides the inspiration or empowerment for the godly action. In other verses, grace works with another of God's expressions for your good. For example, "Grace and Truth," or "Grace and Mercy." In these cases, grace and the other spiritual force are working for your benefit.

We often hear appeals for balance when it comes to biblical teaching, and balance is very important. Keep in mind, however, that true balance is never achieved by combining fifty percent faith with fifty percent unbelief, or fifty percent grace and fifty percent legalism. Rather, we achieve balance when we rightly divide the word of truth (2 Timothy 2:15) and live by every word that proceeds from the mouth of God.

A good physical trainer will work all of the muscle groups of someone who wants to get in shape. Can you imagine a trainer only having a client working on their upper body week after week? If they worked out long enough, the person would probably end up with well-defined muscles above the waist—and skinny little legs! We would question the wisdom of a trainer whose workout regimen developed one part of the client's body and not another part.

If we want to be whole, strong, and effective Christians, we would do well to remember the lesson contained in the following song I learned in childhood. It had several different titles: "Dem Bones," "Dry Bones," or "Dem Dry Bones." It may not have been anatomically correct, but it made the point.

> The foot bone connected to the leg-bone,
> The leg bone connected to the knee bone,
> The knee bone connected to the thigh bone,
> The thigh bone connected to the back bone,
> The back bone connected to the neck bone
> The neck bone connected to the head bone
> Oh hear the word of the Lord! [2]

God doesn't want you to be disjointed. He does not want your perspective of grace to be distorted because you have disconnected it from the other truths He has communicated in His Word. He wants you "together". Then your entire life will be healthy and strong in Him.

Chapter 20

RECOGNIZING OUR FILTERS

True repentance is to cease from sin.

—Ambrose of Milan[1]

When he was very young, my brother Dave was fascinated with electrical outlets. This was before the days of safety plugs, and several times my mom caught him just before he was about to stick something into one. One day she wasn't quick enough. He found a screwdriver that fit nicely into one of the outlet slots and, needless to say, was shocked badly. He was so traumatized that he refused to plug anything into an outlet for years to come. His experience was extremely negative.

Imagine another young boy, who grew up in a home that had all the necessary outlets, but his father never paid the electric bill. No matter what the boy plugged or stuck into those outlets, nothing happened. His experience with them would be much different than my brother's. It would be neutral, neither positive nor negative.

Finally, picture another young boy, who grew up in a home enjoying all the benefits of electricity, and he never did anything that would cause an unpleasant shock. Whatever he plugged in worked, and he enjoyed the benefits of games, television, air conditioning, and all kinds of things run by electricity. As a result, this boy's experience with electrical outlets was very positive.

Each of these three boys, growing up, is going to have a different perspective on electrical outlets based on their experiences. The first is afraid of them because he was severely hurt by one. The second may feel disappointment or complete apathy because his outlets never produced any results. The third child sees the outlets as a great source of help and usefulness.

Likewise, each of us have background experiences or filters through which we process information about life, including our perspective of the Bible. We might like to think we are totally objective when we read Scripture, but in reality it is difficult not to read subjectively, based on our life experiences.

For example, someone who grew up in a home with a father who was abusive, condemning, and critical can find it challenging to relate to God as a Father, who loves them unconditionally. Individuals often share what a great struggle it is for them to refer to God as their Heavenly Father because of painful and traumatic associations with their earthly fathers. We can have empathy in those types of situations, but we can't eradicate all that the Bible says about God as a Father.

Likewise, someone who was subjected to much condemning, legalistic, and guilt-laden preaching will likely have a different perspective of God (at least initially) than someone who who was raised hearing extensively about the love, grace, and mercy of God.

You don't want past experiences to obscure your perception of the truth, but that might mean letting go of some "sacred cows." You cannot hold on to old filters when you realize they obscure the truth of God's Word. On the other hand, you should not assume everything you learned was wrong. Perhaps some of what you discovered or were taught is right in line with what the Bible says. Trust the Holy Spirit to help you "test all things; hold fast what is good" (1 Thessalonians 5:21).

> *Don't suppress the Spirit, and don't stifle those who have a word from the Master. On the other hand, don't be gullible. Check out everything, and keep only what's good. Throw out anything tainted with evil.*
> 1 Thessalonians 5:21-22 MSG

We must be willing to allow the Holy Spirit free reign in how we view things. We must esteem the truth of Scripture to be our guide; not the traditions of man. Keep this idea of filters and truth in mind as we explore one of the issues that works closely with grace: confession.

Confession of Sin, for Example…

When it comes to confession of sin, each of us has a different religious or nonreligious background that affects our perspective. Let's look at some different views of confession. Then we will see what the Bible says about it.

1. Confession of sin is a religious ritual. Some people were raised to go through the motions of religious confession with very little heartfelt involvement. Such formalities became dead works that were performed mechanically and ceremonially. Basically they would recite the prescribed words on a church bulletin or in a confessional to get rid of their guilt until the next time for confession. No doubt many may have done this sincerely, but others confessed their sins routinely, mindlessly, and superficially without it ever impacting their souls. For these individuals, the confession of sin was a lifeless ritual.

2. Confession of sin is an obsession. Some people are naturally conscientious, sensitive, and prone to intense guilt. Such individuals can become religiously preoccupied with confessing every sin, whether real or imagined. They continually feel insecure and distressed about whether

God loves them and forgives them or is displeased and has turned His back on them. They may fear dying without confessing that one last or forgotten sin, which, in their mind, will send them to Hell. This type of person may see God as a sadistic fault-finder, who is eagerly looking to find their sins, so that He can punish them.

These individuals may come to the altar week after week, confessing the same sins over and over again. They continually bemoan their sinfulness and wallow in their unworthiness, trying to show God just how sorry they really are. Then maybe, just maybe, if they put enough remorse and effort into it, God will decide to forgive them.

In their sense of vulnerability, they fall victim to a works mentality in which they are consciously or subconsciously trying to earn God's forgiveness, sometimes frantically so. For these individuals, their continual confession of sin (not the grace of God through Jesus) is what will save them from eternal damnation.

3. Confession of sin is not an issue. Not everyone is sensitive and conscientious. While some are quick to accuse themselves, others are just as quick to excuse themselves. In one ministry organization, the leader would give the employees an occasional pep talk. He expressed appreciation and commended them for working hard, then he mentioned he had noticed some of them were not being as productive as they could be. He exhorted the employees to be more diligent, to pick up the pace, and to hustle to get all their work done.

Inevitably, the hardest working, most diligent, and most sincere employee would be the only one to come up to the leader and say, "Thank you for that encouragement. I promise I'll work harder." He was so conscientious that he believed the exhortation was just for him . Meanwhile, the ones who had been slacking off did not respond at all; the admonition had rolled off them like water off the proverbial duck's back. People tend to hear what they want to hear and not hear what they don't want to hear.

While some are very tenderhearted, conscientious, and quick to apologize; others are calloused, insensitive, and not the least likely to feel remorse or regret over wrong actions. Their response to the confession of sin issue would be simply, "What sin?" Instead of confessing they were a thief, they would believe it was the other person's fault for leaving the item out to tempt them. Instead of confessing they had abused their spouse , they would assume the spouse "had it coming." Instead of confessing they had used vulgar language, they would say, "What's the big deal? Everybody talks that way."

These individuals are so calloused, they see no need to acknowledge or turn from sin.

4. Confession of sin is a meaningful expression of faith. Some people came to understand the unconditional love of God, that His love for them was not based on their perfection or performance. They received illumination concerning redemption by grace through faith, and their conscience was released from their preoccupation with sin and the harsh condemnation brought on by "the accuser of the brethren" (Revelation 12:10).

When such a person comes to a realization of the magnificent forgiveness that is theirs through the Cross and the blood of Jesus, they know Jesus died for their sins, and God forgave them, making them righteous with His righteousness. Now, when they miss it or sin, they know God still loves them and is merciful and forgiving. They easily go to Him, confess their sin in faith, thank Him for forgiving them, and move forward in their life, free from guilt, shame, and condemnation.

Different Experiences, Same Bible

While we all tend to see truth through filters, we need to teach comprehensively from the Word and not make a doctrine out of our own personal experience. Our testimonies can be helpful and provide beneficial insights, especially when they relate to those from a similar background, but ultimately we need to be able to say with the apostle Paul, "We do not preach ourselves, but Christ Jesus the Lord" (2 Corinthians 4:5).

If each of us submits our "filters" and personal experiences to the Word of God—making it the final authority —all of us can have a true, scriptural understanding of the grace of God, regardless of our past.

Chapter 21

Repentance and Confession

An erroneous concept that has crept into the minds of many today involves how grace, repentance, confession, and forgiveness work together in our new life in Jesus Christ. Some have the distinct impression that living under grace means after being saved that it is unnecessary to repent of or confess sins we commit. We simply recognize that we were already forgiven. Before we address this directly, let's define our terms scripturally.

Repentance

The words "repent" and "repentance" are often misunderstood. Let's make sure we know the true, biblical definition of repentance, which is translated from the Greek word *metanoia*. Here is what some of the most respected Greek scholars have to say:

> The Greek noun metanoia literally means, "a change of mind." It is more than an emotional sorrow, which too often does not produce any change of life. Rather, it is a change of mind, or attitude, toward God, sin, and ourselves.
>
> —Ralph Earle[1]

...the change of mind of those who have begun to abhor their errors and misdeeds, and have determined to enter upon a better course of life, so that it embraces both a recognition of sin and sorrow for it and hearty amendment, the tokens and effects of which are good deeds.

—Joseph H. Thayer[2]

In his outstanding work, *A Light in the Darkness: Seven Messages to the Seven Churches*, Rick Renner writes:

The word 'repent' comes from the Greek word *metanoeo*, which is a compound of *meta* and *nous*. The word meta means to turn, and the word nous means one's mind, intellect, will, frame of thinking, opinion, or general view of life. When the words meta and nous are combined together; the new word depicts a decision to completely change the way one thinks, lives, or behaves. This doesn't describe a temporary emotional sorrow for past actions; rather, it is a solid, intellectual decision to turn about-face and take a new direction, to completely alter one's life by discarding an old, destructive pattern and embracing a brand new one. True repentance involves a conscious decision both to turn away from sin, selfishness, and rebellion, and to turn toward God with all of one's heart and mind. It is a complete, 180-degree turn in one's thinking and behaving.[3]

If we don't understand what repentance is, we may think it involves an on-going preoccupation with particular sins we have committed, or that it is simply the decision to abandon certain bad habits. Every December 31, countless people (saved and unsaved alike) make resolutions to eat healthier, to lose weight, to quit smoking or drinking, to be nicer, or to change something else in their lives. While some make good on such resolutions, it is well known that most are notoriously unsuccessful; the vast majority have completely abandoned their resolutions by the end of January.

Resolutions are not the same as repentance. William Douglas Chamberlain wrote, "The Christian faith turns men's faces forward. Repentance is the reorientation of a personality with reference to God and His purpose."[4] Chamberlain proceeded to quote another who suggested an alternative word for repentance: transmentation. He said the word describes "the mental transfiguration which both John and Jesus called for: a transposed mind which thinks new thoughts, aspires for better things, and acknowledges a new sovereignty—God's will, not one's own."[5] Further, he states that in order for believers to enjoy the kingdom of God, they must "undergo a mental transfiguration, which we call 'repentance.' Repentance looks ahead in hope and anticipation while remorse looks backward in shame and forward in fear."[6]

Like grace, repentance involves both attitude and action. There is the discontinuation of wrong behavior based upon a heart and mind that have turned completely toward God and His ways. Repentance does not result from some kind of heavenly slap on the wrist for wrongdoing or being sent to the "time-out" corner. Repentance occurs when our hearts and minds are awakened to God's glorious potential for our lives. In the light of God's goodness and good intentions toward us, we recognize the deficiency of our selfish perspective and the destructiveness of our sinful behavior. Thus, we turn from them in order to embrace a new, better, and higher life offered by a God of grace.

It is unfortunate that repentance has not been well understood. In some churches, the wrong conduct of believers is never addressed for fear of offending people or for fear of being labeled "legalistic." This is sad because the New Testament has much to say about godly and ungodly conduct for Christians. Simultaneously, other believers have been exposed to preaching against sin that is more like being beaten with a club, and of course, great guilt ensues. Without a proper understanding of grace, people may express sorrow for their sins but never find freedom or liberty from them. When the liberating power of God's grace is not proclaimed, believers remain preoccupied with their shortcomings and sins and live perpetually under guilt and condemnation instead of discovering the freedom offered by the Spirit of God.

Grace Consciousness

For the law, having a shadow of the good things to come, and not the very image of the things, can never with these same sacrifices, which they offer continually year by year, make those who approach perfect. For then would they not have ceased to be offered? For **the worshipers, once purified, would have had no more consciousness of sins.** *But in those sacrifices there is a reminder of sins every year. For it is not possible for the blood of bulls and goats to take away sins.*

Hebrews 10:1-4

Under the Old Testament system, believers received a "covering" not a "cleansing." They received an annual "reminder" of sin but not a total "remission" of sin (see also Hebrews 9:9). It was only with the sacrifice of Jesus that believers received complete cleansing and remission of sin. As a result, we do not have to walk around with a "sin consciousness." We do not need to be preoccupied with past faults or live under a shadow of guilt and condemnation. "If the Son makes you free, you shall be free indeed" (John 8:36).

The sacrifices of the Old Testament continually reminded those under the Law that there was an on-going sin issue; the once-for-all sacrifice of the Lord Jesus Christ continually reminds us that we have been cleansed and made righteous. His blood has fully washed us and made us pure, and we no longer need to live under guilt, condemnation, or preoccupation with sin.

Having no more consciousness of sin, however, does not mean we are insensitive or take lightly sins we might commit as a believer. It simply means we no longer walk around under a cloud of guilt, shame, and condemnation—as though our sins had not been forgiven. Moreover, if and when we do sin, we don't need to walk around berating and condemning ourselves, but we turn once again to God, acknowledge our sin and turn from it, re-focus and move forward with God, knowing that He has forgiven us our sin and cleansed us from all unrighteousness. To respond to God in such a way is not walking in "sin-consciousness." Rather, it is walking in "grace consciousness" that enables us to know that we can, "... come boldly to the throne of grace, that we may obtain mercy and find grace to help in time of need" (Hebrews 4:16).

True Confessions

If we confess our sins, He is faithful and just to forgive us our sins and to cleanse us from all unrighteousness.

1 John 1:9

Previously I used confession as an example of how our past experiences can filter our perspective and beliefs about various doctrinal issues. We saw how confession can mean different things to different people. In the Bible, "confess" is translated from the Greek word *homologeo*, which is derived from *homou* (the same) and *lego* (to say). Hence, it is typically defined as meaning to speak the same thing. Confess also means to consent, admit, agree, concede, and to acknowledge.[7] Commenting on the word confess in 1 John 1:9, *The Bible Exposition Commentary* says,

To confess sins means much more than simply to "admit" them. The word confess actually means "to say the same thing [about]." To confess sin, then, means to say the same thing about it that God says about it. True confession is naming sin—calling it by name what God calls it: envy, hatred, lust, deceit, or whatever it may be. Confession simply means being honest with ourselves and with God, and if others are involved, being honest with them too. It is more than admitting sin. It means judging sin and facing it squarely.[8]

After Hezekiah "turned his face to the wall" and prayed, God said, "I have heard your prayer, I have seen your tears; surely I will heal you" (2 Kings 20:5). In this case, Hezekiah's tears represented the sincere and heartfelt nature of his confession of sin and repentance. David said, "You keep track of all my sorrows. You have collected all my tears in your bottle. You have recorded each one in your book" (Psalm 56:8).

On the other hand in Malachi 2:13, God noted the tears of those who prayed, but He was unimpressed due to the perpetual rebellion and disobedience of the people. They cried over their situation, not that their hearts were far from Him. God is compassionate, but tears or emotions, in and of themselves, do not move Him; Jesus never said, "According to your emotionalism be it unto you." What He said was, "According to your faith be it unto you" (Matthew 9:29 KJV). Simple trust is what pleases Him.

If you have an emotional response to God that is heartfelt and genuine, that's great, but you should never feel like God will hear you better or respond more favorably if you work yourself into an emotional state. We need to be sincere and honest with God, knowing that His grace will be poured through our repentance the same way we were saved: through faith.

Under the Old Covenant

One of the major functions of the Old Testament prophets was to call God's people to turn from sin and return to God. Of course, God wanted His people to have faith in Him, but He also knew authentic faith is reflected in corresponding actions. He did not want lip service from His people; He wanted hearts that were surrendered to Him and lives that were responsive to His will.

If you read through the Old Testament prophets, you will see dozens of instances of God's people repenting and confessing their sins. Here's one example from Jeremiah:

> *The LORD gave another message to Jeremiah. He said, "Go to the entrance of the LORD's Temple, and give this message to the people: 'O Judah, listen to this message from the LORD! Listen to it, all of you who worship here! This is what the LORD of Heaven's Armies, the God of Israel, says:*
>
> *"'Even now, if you quit your evil ways, I will let you stay in your own land. But don't be fooled by those who promise you safety simply because the LORD's Temple is here. They chant, "The LORD's Temple is here! The LORD's Temple is here!" But I will be merciful only if you stop your evil thoughts and deeds and start treating each other with justice; only if you stop exploiting foreigners, orphans, and widows; only if you stop your murdering; and only if you stop harming yourselves by worshiping idols. Then I will let you stay in this land that I gave to your ancestors to keep forever.*
>
> *"'Don't be fooled into thinking that you will never suffer because the Temple is here. It's a lie! Do you really think you can steal, murder, commit adultery, lie, and burn incense to Baal and all those other new gods of yours, and then come here and stand before me in my Temple and chant, "We are safe!"—only to go right back to all those evils again? Don't you yourselves admit that this Temple, which bears my name, has become a den of thieves? Surely I see all the evil going on there. I, the LORD, have spoken!"*

Jeremiah 7:1-11 NLT

Powerful stuff! God obviously was not impressed with feigned words or empty promises, nor did He ignore their sin and idolatry just because they went to the Temple regularly to go through the religious rituals. He wanted to see genuine, heartfelt confession and repentance. The Old Testament reveals a long-standing heritage of confession and repentance, both by individuals and the nation as a whole. These were sacred and defining moments in Israel's history, serving as landmark events that were greatly honored and blessed by God. As the Holy Spirit inspired the recording of Scripture, He ensured these were recorded for the benefit of all generations of believers. Here are a few examples:

Moses—Under the Levitical priesthood, the confession of sin was part of a ceremony in which the sins of the people were symbolically transferred to a goat, which was sent into the wilderness. The goat represented the Messiah and foreshadowed how Jesus would literally take away the sin of the world.

When Aaron has finished purifying the Most Holy Place and the Tabernacle and the altar, he must present the live goat. He will lay both of his hands on the goat's head and confess over it all the wickedness, rebellion, and sins of the people of Israel. In this way, he will transfer the people's sins to the head of the goat. Then a man specially chosen for the task will drive the goat into the wilderness. As the goat goes into the wilderness, it will carry all the people's sins upon itself into a desolate land.

Leviticus 16:20-22 NLT

David—"I have sinned greatly in what I have done; but now, I pray, O Lord, take away the iniquity of Your servant, for I have done very foolishly" (2 Samuel 24:10). Like Psalm 32:5 says,

I acknowledged my sin to You,
And my iniquity I have not hidden.
I said, "I will confess my transgressions to the Lord,"
And You forgave the iniquity of my sin.

Additional confessions by David and other psalmists can be found in Psalm 38:18, Psalm 41:4, Psalm 51:2-4, Psalm 106:6, and many more. David also said, "If I had not confessed the sin in my heart, the Lord would not have listened" (Psalm 66:18 NLT). Other translations of this verse read:

- "If I had been cozy with evil, the Lord would never have listened" (MSG).

- "If I had cherished sin in my heart, the Lord would not have listened" (NIV[11]).

- "If I regard iniquity in my heart, the Lord will not hear me" (AMP).

Solomon—"He who covers his sins will not prosper, But whoever confesses and forsakes them will have mercy" (Proverbs 28:13; see also 1 Kings 8:46-50).

Ezra— Ezra 9:6 shows the prophet confessing: "O my God, I am too ashamed and humiliated to lift up my face to You, my God; for our iniquities have risen higher than our heads, and our guilt has grown up to the heavens" (paraphrase mine). We also see Ezra leading corporate repentance among God's people: "Now while Ezra was praying, and while he was confessing, weeping, and bowing down before the house of God, a very large assembly of men, women, and children gathered to him from Israel; for the people wept very bitterly" (Ezra 10:1).

Nehemiah—"...that You may hear the prayer of Your servant which I pray before You now, day and night, for the children of Israel Your servants, and confess the sins of the children of Israel which we have sinned against You. Both my father's house and I have sinned. We have acted very corruptly against You, and have not kept the commandments, the statutes, nor the ordinances which You commanded Your servant Moses" (Nehemiah 1:6-7).

Just as Ezra had done, Nehemiah also led the people of God in corporate repentance: "And they stood and confessed their sins and the iniquities of their fathers. And they stood up in their place and read from the Book of the Law of the Lord their God for one-fourth of the day; and for another fourth they confessed and worshiped the Lord their God" (Nehemiah 9:2-3).

Isaiah—This great prophet of Israel acknowledged his own sin and the sin of his people. "So I said: 'Woe is me, for I am undone! Because I am a man of unclean lips, And I dwell in the midst of a people of unclean lips; For my eyes have seen the King, The Lord of hosts'" (Isaiah 6:5). He later wrote, "For our transgressions are multiplied before You, and our sins testify against us" (Isaiah 59:12).

Jeremiah—"We acknowledge, O Lord, our wickedness And the iniquity of our fathers, For we have sinned against You" (Jeremiah 14:20).

Daniel—"We have sinned and committed iniquity, we have done wickedly and rebelled, even by departing from Your precepts and Your judgments. Neither have we heeded Your servants the prophets" (Daniel 9:5-6). Chapter 9 of Daniel is entirely devoted to Daniel's confession and repentance, and also details God's response through a visitation by the angel Gabriel.

Throughout Israel's history, whenever there was sincere repentance and confession from the people, God responded with mercy, forgiveness, and compassion. David's realization certainly proved to be true: "The sacrifices of God are a broken spirit, A broken and a contrite heart—These, O God, You will not despise" (Psalm 51:17).

Isaiah expressed this beautiful decree:

> *Let the wicked forsake his way,*
>
> *And the unrighteous man his thoughts;*
>
> *Let him return to the Lord,*

And He will have mercy on him;

And to our God,

For He will abundantly pardon.

Isaiah 55:7

John the Baptist—By the time John the Baptist came on the scene, the nation of Israel was very familiar with the idea of repentance and confession, and John had a simple message: "Repent, for the kingdom of heaven is at hand!" (Matthew 3:2). Masses of people responded. Matthew 3:5-6 says, "Then Jerusalem, all Judea, and all the region around the Jordan went out to him and were baptized by him in the Jordan, confessing their sins." He also exhorted his listeners to "bear fruits worthy of repentance" (Matthew 3:8).

In response to John's exhortation that repentance be tangibly expressed by fruit, or a corresponding lifestyle change, the people asked John what they should do (Luke 3:10). John responded by letting them know that true repentance would be evidenced by godly behavior.

> *He answered and said to them, "He who has two tunics, let him give to him who has none; and he who has food, let him do likewise."*
>
> *Then tax collectors also came to be baptized, and said to him, "Teacher, what shall we do?"*
>
> *And he said to them, "Collect no more than what is appointed for you."*
>
> *Likewise the soldiers asked him, saying, "And what shall we do?"*
>
> *So he said to them, "Do not intimidate anyone or accuse falsely, and be content with your wages."*

Luke 3:11-14

In the Old Testament, repentance from and confession of sin was a rich part of Israel's journey with God. Repentance and confession was not viewed as a negative thing but a positive change that would restore the people to God and release His blessings. They were not simply turning away from sin; they were turning their hearts back to God. In turn, He poured out His grace and blessing time and time again. The people learned that when they sinned, they didn't need to throw themselves upon their swords; they needed to throw themselves upon His mercy in faith that He would give them a new beginning and new hope.

Chapter 22

What Did Jesus Say?

With the confession of sin and repentance being such an intrinsic and enduring part of Jewish history, what did Jesus say about it? He certainly didn't need to introduce the concept to anyone—it was already firmly established in the hearts and minds of the people. Did He reinforce the idea of confession and repentance, or did He eradicate it? Consider what Jesus taught and how He interacted with people:

Jesus' First Sermon: The very first words Jesus preached (according to Matthew 4:17) were "Repent, for the kingdom of heaven is at hand." Mark 1:15 records Jesus' first message as, "The time is fulfilled, and the kingdom of God is at hand. Repent, and believe in the gospel." Jesus later said, "I have not come to call the righteous, but sinners, to repentance" (Luke 5:32).

The Preaching of the Disciples: When Jesus sent out the disciples two by two to minister, Mark 6:12 tells us, "So they went out and preached that people should repent."

The Lord's Prayer: When His disciples asked Him to teach them to pray, Jesus taught them what is considered the model prayer. Included within that prayer is the following statement: "And forgive us our sins, For we also forgive everyone who is indebted to us" (Luke 11:4).

The Story of the Prodigal Son: The acknowledgement, confession, and repentance from sin plays an important theme in one of the most beloved stories Jesus ever told. In returning to his father, the prodigal son says, "Father, I have sinned against heaven and in your sight, and am no longer worthy to be called your son" (Luke 15:21, see also 15:18-19). He was going to request that he be taken back merely as a hired servant, but he underestimated the depth and magnitude of his father's love. As we read the entire story in Luke 15:11-32, we see how eager the father was to bestow his love and forgiveness on this erring son long before he ever returned; his father had never stopped loving him. Hence, the young man was received not as a hired servant but as a celebrated son. It would seem strange that Jesus would present this beautiful depiction of the father's love and grace, as well as the son's repentance and confession, if these were not valuable components in the restoration process of a believer who had gone astray.

The Woman Caught in Adultery: Jesus was full of grace when He told the woman in John 8:11, "Neither do I condemn you," but He also told her, "Go and sin no more." He dealt with both sides of the coin. He did not give her a directive for future behavior without releasing her from past condemnation, neither did He release her from past condemnation without giving her direction for future behavior.

The Infirm Man: Jesus said to the man who had been infirm for thirty-eight years, "See, you have been made well. Sin no more, lest a worse thing come upon you" (John 5:14). Jesus imparted mercy, grace, forgiveness, and redemption, and certainly all these things are free gifts, unearned and undeserved. At the same time, we can readily see that He had no problem telling people to stop sinful behavior.

The Great Commission: In Luke 24:47, Jesus commissioned the disciples by saying, "...that repentance and remission of sins should be preached in His name to all nations, beginning at Jerusalem."

After His Ascension: Someone might say, "Yes, but all that had to do with people who were not born again, so they needed to repent. But

Christians, once they are forgiven, don't really need to repent or confess their sins again because Jesus has taken care of them." This opinion ignores numerous New Testament scriptures, including how Jesus addressed erring believers in Revelation 2-3:

- To the Christians in Ephesus: "Remember therefore from where you have fallen; repent and do the first works, or else I will come to you quickly and remove your lamp stand from its place—unless you repent" (Revelation 2:5).

- To the Christians in Pergamos: "Repent, or else I will come to you quickly and will fight against them with the sword of My mouth" (Revelation 2:16).

- To the Christians in Thyatira: "And I gave her time to repent of her sexual immorality, and she did not repent. Indeed I will cast her into a sickbed, and those who commit adultery with her into great tribulation, unless they repent of their deeds" (Revelation 2:21-22).

- To the Christians in Sardis: "Remember therefore how you have received and heard; hold fast and repent. Therefore if you will not watch, I will come upon you as a thief, and you will not know what hour I will come upon you" (Revelation 3:3).

- To the Christians in Laodicea: "As many as I love, I rebuke and chasten. Therefore be zealous and repent" (Revelation 3:19)

In these passages Jesus is speaking to believers, who were born again and had put their faith and trust in Him. Nevertheless, He commanded them to repent, awaken to His goodness, change their direction, and bring their lives into divine order. He didn't say, "You're already forgiven, so you don't need to repent or confess anything." Neither did He tell them to repent so they could earn their forgiveness.

In these churches, their lives, their belief-systems, their attitudes, and their conduct had become badly distorted. They had lost sight of the Lord's will and purpose in certain areas of their lives and the life of their church. There were major adjustments that needed to be made, and Jesus unapologetically told them to repent. Keep in mind that repentance isn't just dealing with past failures, but it is calling people from those past failures to God's higher plan for their future.

When considering this question of why we have to repent and confess our sins if forgiveness has already been provided on the Cross, we certainly cannot minimize the significance of the spiritual realities that are ours through Christ. But God wants more than a legal contract with us; He desires intimate fellowship and communion with us, as well as obedience from us.

You Wouldn't Treat Your Spouse the Way Some Treat God

The idea has been presented, "You don't need to confess your sins to God in order to be forgiven; He has already forgiven you." While there is some truth in that statement, it can also be misleading. It is true that legally, our sins were forgiven on the Cross, but if a husband used that logic in his marriage he would conclude, "When I've offended my wife, I don't need to apologize to her in order to be married." That may be true in a sense, but this gross insensitivity and lack of communication would seriously damage the relationship. It would be foolish for a man who has offended his wife to hold up their marriage license and say, "Honey, my behavior doesn't need to be addressed because we were legally married years ago, and you said you accepted me 'for better or worse.'"

If a husband desires to honor and respect his wife, he should apologize and let her know that he doesn't want to hurt her again by insensitive actions or words. It is one thing to be legally married; it is another thing to love and honor each other for the commitment you have made. If the husband respects his legal covenant of marriage, he will also realize there is an experiential, practical, and communicative part of it. He needs to do right by his wife to keep their relationship vibrant and healthy.

Throughout the Bible, the Holy Spirit uses the marriage covenant symbolically as a type of our relationship with the Lord Jesus Christ, so should we treat Him with less consideration than we would our spouse? We certainly do not earn our salvation by repenting and confessing our sins to Jesus, and repentance and confession in no way takes the place of Jesus' redemptive work; but when we sin, the biblically prescribed way of interacting with God is to repent of and confess our sin to Him. This is the divinely ordained way of expressing our faith to receive and appropriate the forgiveness Jesus made legally available to us when He shed His blood, died on the Cross, and rose again.

God Wants Meaningful Interaction

In Matthew 6:7, Jesus instructed His disciples not to "use vain repetitions as the heathen do," but encouraged them to pray in direct, simple, and clear terms. He said, "Your Father knows the things you have need of before you ask Him" (Matthew 6:8). This may beg the question, "If He knows what we need before we ask Him, why should we ask?" Again, the answer is that God wants us to relate to Him in faith, based on His Word. He wants more than a legal union with us; He desires a truly interactive and intimate relationship with us. James took this further when he wrote, "You do not have because you do not ask" (James 4:2).

In discussing repentance and confession, "asking" certainly does not mean we make ignorant and uninformed inquiries of God. We don't beg Him to forgive us as though we are uncertain as to whether He will or not; He has already provided forgiveness and extended His grace through what Jesus did. The joy of trusting God and believing His Word is that we know what His response will be before we approach Him. When we have missed it, we don't approach God with uncertainty and doubt, as though He were undependable, unreliable, or unwilling to fulfill His promises. Instead, we do exactly what Scripture tells us to do. We "come boldly to the throne of our gracious God. There we will receive his mercy, and we will find grace to help us when we need it most" (Hebrews 4:16 NLT).

Chapter 23

WHAT DID THE APOSTLES SAY?

Paul

Many who became **believers confessed their sinful practices.** *A number of them who had been practicing sorcery brought their incantation books and burned them at a public bonfire. The value of the books was several million dollars.*

Acts 19:18-19 NLT (bold mine)

Those influenced by Paul's ministry demonstrated that believing the gospel and becoming a follower of Jesus produced a lifestyle change. When Paul reviewed his ministry with the Ephesian elders, he said his message was one of, "repentance toward God and faith toward our Lord Jesus Christ" (Acts 20:21).

Paul's statement is extremely important. Did you notice he said, "repentance toward God?" Remember, healthy repentance isn't simply discontinuing certain behaviors or dropping a bad habit; it is a radical awakening toward God! If all you do is focus on what you are leaving behind, the attraction of those things will be all the more intense. But if you fix your gaze upon the One you are moving toward, you will find yourself drawn toward a life far more wonderful than anything in your past. Paul said, "But one thing I do, forgetting those things which are behind and reaching forward to those things which are ahead" (Philippians 3:13).

Remember the words to the old song: "Turn your eyes upon Jesus, Look full in His wonderful face, And the things of Earth will grow strangely dim, In the light of His glory and grace."[1] In Romans 2:4, Paul taught that God's goodness leads us to repentance. He knew we could see God's goodness as being both the basis and object of our repentance. In other words, when we miss it, the foundation of God's goodness inspires and encourages us to turn from our error, and His goodness is what we turn toward.

The Corinthian believers had apparently become entangled in relationships that were dragging them down spiritually. Though Paul does not use the word repent in the following passage of Scripture, what he advises them to do is a perfect description of repentance.

> *Do not be so deceived and misled! Evil companionships (communion, associations) corrupt and deprave good manners and morals and character.*
>
> **Awake [from your drunken stupor and return] to sober sense and your right minds, and sin no more.**
>
> 1 Corinthians 15:33-34 AMP

The New King James Version of Romans 15:33 says, "Awake to righteousness, and do not sin." Paul could have just told them to stop sinning, but he realized that any lasting change in outward behavior needs to be undergirded by insight into truth, or an awakening unto righteousness. That's why Paul not only told the Romans to present their bodies to God, but also to be transformed by the renewing of their minds (Romans 12:1-2).

> Repentance is to have a twofold issue: reformation in conduct, and transformation of mental outlook.
>
> —William Douglas Chamberlain[2]

Paul told the Athenians, "God overlooked people's ignorance about these things in earlier times, but now he commands everyone everywhere to repent of their sins and turn to him" (Acts 17:30 NLT). In describing his ministry to King Agrippa, he said: "I preached...that all must repent of their sins and turn to God—and prove they have changed by the good things they do" (Acts 26:20 NLT). The Amplified Bible renders that passage, "...that they should repent and turn to God, and do works and live lives consistent with and worthy of their repentance."

In all these verses, Paul indicates that repentance isn't simply feeling bad about past mistakes, but also it works hand-in-hand with turning toward God to change your life.

A Pauline Case Study of Repentance

Paul vividly and powerfully addresses the confession of and repentance from sin among the believers in Corinth in what is perhaps his most emotionally charged and candid piece of correspondence. After a very painful visit with them, he decided to write them a very strong letter instead of coming to see them again. He said, "The reason I didn't return to Corinth was to spare you from a severe rebuke" (2 Corinthians 1:23 NLT).

Having gone into Macedonia (northern Greece), Paul faced enormous problems and pressures, and the uncertainty of how the Corinthians would respond to his "severe" letter to them weighed heavily on him. Titus came to Paul from Corinth and reported that the Corinthians had repented, which brought great joy and relief to Paul's heart. Instead of driving the Corinthians away, his rebuke had produced the desired results in the hearts and lives of those believers.

Paul let the Corinthians know what he went through on their behalf, and how proud he was of them:

I wrote that letter in great anguish, with a troubled heart and many tears. I didn't want to grieve you, but I wanted to let you know how much love I have for you.

2 Corinthians 2:4 NLT

God, who encourages those who are discouraged, encouraged us by the arrival of Titus. His presence was a joy, but so was the news he brought of the encouragement he received from you. When he told us how much you long to see me, and **how sorry you are for what happened,** *and how loyal you are to me, I was filled with joy!*

I am not sorry that I sent that **severe letter** *to you, though I was sorry at first, for I know it was* **painful** *to you for a little while. Now I am glad I sent it, not because it hurt you, but because* **the pain caused you to repent and change your ways. It was the kind of sorrow God wants his people to have,** *so you were not harmed by us in any way. For* **the kind of sorrow God wants us to experience leads us away from sin and results in salvation.** *There's no regret for that kind of sorrow. But worldly sorrow, which lacks repentance, results in spiritual death.*

Just **see what this godly sorrow produced in you***! Such earnestness, such concern to clear yourselves, such indignation, such alarm, such longing to see me, such zeal, and such a readiness to punish wrong. You showed that* **you have done everything necessary to make things right.**

2 Corinthians 7:6-11 NLT (bold mine)

The Message renders verse 11, "And now, isn't it wonderful all the ways in which this distress has goaded you closer to God? You're more alive, more concerned, more sensitive, more reverent, more human, more passionate, more responsible. Looked at from any angle, you've come out of this with purity of heart."

Paul commended these believers for taking their error seriously, turning away from sin in an intentional and meaningful way, and thus producing godly fruit. He described their sorrow as "godly" because of their awakening to the holiness of God, which naturally produced repentance and confession of their sin, followed by a transformation that immediately began to produce good fruit in their lives.

I propose that confession of sin is an integral, inseparable, and foundational part of repentance. How can a person turn away from something negative and toward something positive unless he acknowledges the negative (sin) that he is turning from and the positive (God) that he is turning toward? When a person confesses a sin, they are honestly acknowledging they have missed it, agreeing with God's assessment of the situation, and conceding to obey Him. This is what "confess" means: to acknowledge, to agree with, and to concede.

I believe some Christians are throwing out confession of sin for two reasons. They believe it is not necessary to maintain a right relationship with God. After all, they reason, He has already forgiven them because of the Cross, so why confess a sin God has already forgiven? Also, they believe confessing sin is being sin-conscious but that God has called us to be righteousness-conscious. The first reason does not line up with the example of Paul and the Corinthians, nor does it track with the whole counsel of God on the subject of confession. Confession tells our flesh, "No more! I agree with God!" When confession is made to a person (James 5:16) as well as to God, this lets at least one other person know, so they can pray for them and help hold them accountable.

To address the second reason, to confess sin does not mean to continually dwell on sin. It is an honest acknowledgement before God that is made to reorient ourselves to obedience. Because forgiveness is received, there is no need to continually rehash the sin issue before God. There is no doubt, however, that Paul was adamant that believers repent of their sins:

For I am afraid that when I come I won't like what I find, and you won't like my response. I am afraid that I will find quarreling, jealousy, anger, selfishness, slander, gossip, arrogance, and disorderly behavior.

Yes, I am afraid that when I come again, God will humble me in your presence. And **I will be grieved because many of you have not given up your old sins. You have not repented** *of your impurity, sexual immorality, and eagerness for lustful pleasure.*

2 Corinthians 12:20-21 NLT (bold mine)

Paul encouraged the believers in Galatia to help each other be restored to the holiness of God and repent; thereby turning away from all carnality and ungodly behavior.

Brethren, if any person is overtaken in misconduct or sin of any sort, you who are spiritual [who are responsive to and controlled by the Spirit] should set him right and restore and reinstate him, without any sense of superiority and with all gentleness, keeping an attentive eye on yourself, lest you should be tempted also.

Galatians 6:1 AMP

It is not merely our responsibility to cultivate and steward our own personal walk with God, but we have a responsibility, according to Paul, to endeavor to help others in their walk with God as well. God intended for His family to be a caring community on the Earth, in which the members cheered each other on in their respective journeys. Ecclesiastes 4:9-10 NLT illustrates the power of partnership beautifully when it says, "Two people are better off than one, for they can help each other succeed. If one person falls, the other can reach out and help. But someone who falls alone is in real trouble."

Of course, we are never truly alone when the Lord is with us, but it is important to be vitally connected with other members of the body of

Christ. Let's not just be recipients of God's grace in our own personal lives, but let's become distributors of His grace toward others as well. This is not just a good idea or a vague possibility; it is God's determined plan for our lives. God's grace doesn't drive us into isolation; His grace leads us into vital, life-giving, mutually beneficial relationships with one another. Paul knew that God's grace functioned most powerfully when the saints were open and honest not only with God, but with each other as well. I believe God smiles upon gracious believers helping one another in compassion and wisdom to live holy, fruitful, and productive lives.

James

James, the Lord's brother, spoke with authority and conviction when he addressed Christians whose walk with God was not what it should be. This early Church leader was very concerned about believers who had compromised their faith and had become worldly (see James 4:4). His strong admonitions reinforce the significance of repentance in the lives of believers when they get off-track spiritually.

> *Draw near to God and He will draw near to you. Cleanse your hands, you sinners; and purify your hearts, you double-minded. Lament and mourn and weep! Let your laughter be turned to mourning and your joy to gloom. Humble yourselves in the sight of the Lord, and He will lift you up.*
>
> James 4:8-10

Like Paul, James advocated believers helping each other get back on track:

> *Confess your trespasses to one another, and pray for one another, that you may be healed. The effective, fervent prayer of a righteous man avails much.*

Brethren, if anyone among you wanders from the truth, and someone turns him back, let him know that he who turns a sinner from the error of his way will save a soul from death and cover a multitude of sins.

James 5:16,19-20

Did you notice what James said? It is the erring believer coming back that brings about the forgiveness of many sins. Someone might protest, "That can't be right! All of our sins were forgiven when Jesus died on the Cross. Confessing or repenting of sin doesn't cause us to earn our forgiveness." Legally, all of our sins were imputed to Jesus on the Cross, and He procured our forgiveness; but forgiveness is not received by the believer until it is received by the believer!

Teaching that Jesus died for past, present, and future sins is true in a legal sense. This is why Jesus doesn't need to go back to the Cross and die every time someone commits a sin (Hebrews 7:27, 9:12, and 10:10 NLT). It is true that He paid the price for sin once and for all. People though, can greatly misconstrue the application side of this teaching (that Jesus died for all sins: past, present, and future). If a man is found guilty of armed robbery and is pardoned by the judge (or governor), he is only pardoned for that particular offense. The judicial system does not hand the freed man a pass that releases him from the consequences of all future crimes as well. Jesus died for all sins on the Cross, but in no way should that minimize or negate the importance of confession and repentance as the scripturally prescribed means of receiving (not earning) that forgiveness. We cannot replace solid New Testament teaching with the idea that forgiveness is automatically received and experienced (carte blanche) by an individual just because it was purchased by Jesus.

Think back to before you were born again. Even though Jesus had died for your sins, you still had to receive salvation by faith. If a faith response is the means to receive salvation initially, then it seems totally reasonable and scripturally logical for us to again respond in faith (confession and repentance) to receive forgiveness when individual sins are committed currently and in the future.

When we act on God's word in this way and receive His mercy afresh and anew, we are honoring the once-for-all redemptive work of the Lord Jesus. We are honest with God and acknowledge that sin has occurred, but we realize that His love, His mercy, and the cleansing power of the blood of Jesus is greater than any transgression we have committed.

We are never to be flippant or casual about sin, because it is what caused Jesus to undergo the unthinkable suffering He endured for all of us. We should not be glib or nonchalant about something that cost Jesus so dearly.

Peter

True repentance hates the sin, and not merely the penalty; and it hates the sin most of all because it has discovered and felt God's love.

—W. M. Taylor[3]

The Lord's most outspoken disciple, Peter, certainly understood what it meant to sin and to be restored. Jesus told Peter at the Last Supper that he would deny Him later that night. We should never use this as a pretext to deliberately sin, but it is comforting to know that Jesus knew all about the mistakes Peter would be making, yet He loved him, prayed for him, and called him to serve Him anyway.

"Simon, Simon, Satan has asked to sift each of you like wheat. But I have pleaded in prayer for you, Simon, that your faith should not fail. **So when you have repented and turned to me again, strengthen your brothers."***

Peter said, "Lord, I am ready to go to prison with you, and even to die with you."

But Jesus said, "Peter, let me tell you something. Before the rooster crows
tomorrow morning, you will deny three times that you even know me."

Luke 22:31-34 NLT (bold mine)

After his arrest, Peter denied Jesus exactly as predicted.

And the Lord turned and looked at Peter. Then Peter remembered the
word of the Lord, how He had said to him, "Before the rooster crows,
you will deny Me three times." So Peter went out and wept bitterly.

Luke 22:61-62

After His resurrection and before He ascended, Jesus interacted with Peter face-to-face in a way that allowed Peter to reaffirm His love for Jesus three times (the same number of times he had denied knowing Jesus) and to receive a fresh commissioning of His assignment. I encourage you to read this entire encounter in John 21:1-19.

Later in his ministry, Peter had some interesting things to say to a man named Simon the Sorcerer. Simon had been impacted by Philip the evangelist's ministry in Samaria. Acts 8:13 NLT says, "Then Simon himself believed and was baptized. He began following Philip wherever he went, and he was amazed by the signs and great miracles Philip performed." This newly baptized believer still had some very carnal and distorted ideas, and he offered Peter money in order to obtain the ability to impart the Holy Spirit to others. Part of Peter's rebuke to Simon was,

Repent of your wickedness and pray to the Lord. Perhaps he will for-
give your evil thoughts, for I can see that you are full of bitter jealousy
and are held captive by sin.

Acts 8:22-23 NLT

We could say, "Wow! Peter received mercy from the Lord, but he wasn't very merciful toward Simon." It's important to realize that Simon's level of deception was so intense, it probably required a very stern reprimand to wake him up. The apostle Jude indicated that different types of people seem to require different types of approaches in order to secure the proper results.

> *On some have compassion, making a distinction; but others save with*
> *fear, pulling them out of the fire, hating even the garment defiled by*
> *the flesh.*
>
> Jude 22-23

A soft, gentle, "God loves you, Simon," apparently wasn't what he needed to break through the perilous deception that was about to lead him down a very destructive path.

Paul admonished the Romans to "consider the goodness and severity of God" (Romans 11:22). Remember that if God is severe or stern in confronting us about a problem in our life, it is not because He hates us; it is because He loves us. It is not because He lacks grace but because He is so gracious that He is willing "to get in our face" to keep us from destroying ourselves. Jesus said,

> *Those whom I [dearly and tenderly] love, I tell their faults and convict*
> *and convince and reprove and chasten [I discipline and instruct them].*
> *So be enthusiastic and in earnest and burning with zeal and repent*
> *[changing your mind and attitude].*
>
> Revelation 3:19 AMP

This type of correction and training is perfectly consistent with the instruction given in Hebrews 12:5-12, where we are told not to despise but to gladly receive the chastening of the Lord. We are to receive God's correction and training with joy, knowing He corrects us because He loves us and wants us to be "partakers of His holiness" (Hebrews 12:10).

John

When John is mentioned relative to this topic, we naturally think of 1 John 1:9, but let's read this verse in the context of John's comments in chapter 3:

> *See how very much our Father loves us, for he calls us his children, and that is what we are! But the people who belong to this world don't recognize that we are God's children because they don't know him. Dear friends, we are already God's children, but he has not yet shown us what we will be like when Christ appears. But we do know that we will be like him, for we will see him as he really is. And all who have this eager expectation will keep themselves pure, just as he is pure.*
>
> *Everyone who sins is breaking God's law, for all sin is contrary to the law of God. And you know that Jesus came to take away our sins, and there is no sin in him. Anyone who continues to live in him will not sin. But anyone who keeps on sinning does not know him or understand who he is.*
>
> *Dear children, don't let anyone deceive you about this: When people do what is right, it shows that they are righteous, even as Christ is righteous. But when people keep on sinning, it shows that they belong to the devil, who has been sinning since the beginning. But the Son of God came to destroy the works of the devil. Those who have been born into God's family do not make a practice of sinning, because God's life is in them. So they can't keep on sinning, because they are children of God.*
>
> 1 John 3:1-9 NLT

Verse 3 describes our eager expectation of Christ's appearance and our ultimate "transformation," which will be the resurrection of our bodies. This expectation, to be like Jesus (without any desire to sin, without the nature of the flesh) and to know Him fully, inspires us to keep ourselves pure.

In verse 4 John says that sin is contrary to and breaks God's law. John was probably not referencing the Mosaic Law in this statement. When Paul spoke of ministering to Gentiles who did not follow the Mosaic Law, he said, "I too live apart from that law so I can bring them to Christ. But I do not ignore the law of God; I obey the law of Christ" (1 Corinthians 9:21 NLT).

Christians are not under the Mosaic Law, but that does not mean we are lawless. First John 3:4 reads, "Whoever commits sin also commits lawlessness, and sin is lawlessness." Christians are under a new law; it is not one that brings bondage, but one that truly liberates us. We live by the Law of Love! James referred to "the perfect law of liberty" (James 1:25; see also 2:12) and to the royal law (James 2:8), which he said was, "You shall love your neighbor as yourself."

First John 3:6-9 makes it clear that believers should live righteously; they should not make a practice of sinning. In the midst of this exhortation, John makes the statement, "Dear children, don't let anyone deceive you about this" (verse 7). Apparently, there were some false ideas that were attempting to influence John's audience. His remarks seem to indicate that there was an attempt to convince Christians that their behavior did not matter, but John obviously believed otherwise.

Was John promoting the idea that a believer can get to the point in this life that he absolutely never misses it, to a point of sinless perfection? If so, he would seem to be at variance with James' honest acknowledgement (James 3:2):

- "Indeed, we all make many mistakes" (NLT).

- "We all stumble in many ways" (NIV).

- "We all often stumble and fall and offend in many things" (AMP).

Hebrews 12:1 also recognizes human vulnerability with the phrase, "the sin which so easily ensnares us." And lest believers begin to become arrogant in believing in their own flawlessness and infallibility, Paul warned in 1 Corinthians 10:12 AMP, "Therefore let anyone who thinks he stands [who feels sure that he has a steadfast mind and is standing firm], take heed lest he fall [into sin]." The Message version paraphrases it, "Don't be so naive and self-confident. You're not exempt. You could fall flat on your face as easily as anyone else. Forget about self-confidence; it's useless. Cultivate God-confidence."

While the apostle John strongly articulated that believers did not make a practice of sinning, he still recognized our fallibility and let us know that if we do sin, all is not lost and we are not without hope.

My little children, these things I write to you, so that you may not sin. And if anyone sins, we have an Advocate with the Father, Jesus Christ the righteous.

1 John 2:1

Thank God He does not turn against us if we sin! He still loves us and is actively for us. The term "Advocate" can refer to a defense attorney. When Satan and our sins testify against us, Jesus speaks on our behalf, not falsely proclaiming our perfection but truthfully proclaiming His own efficacious work on our behalf. His body and His blood, represented by the elements in communion, are the key witnesses called to testify for us.

Don't Sin, But If You Do...

We saw in 1 John 3 that the practice of sin does not characterize a believer's life, and John makes it clear that he does not want believers to sin. However, he includes, "but if you do sin," and provides believers with clear guidelines on how to receive God's forgiveness and obtain a brand new start. John was not writing to encourage sin, but he desired to obliterate any sense of shame, discouragement, or condemnation that might drive a believer into hopelessness, fear, or despair after missing it.

Satan will either try to get you to have a loose attitude about sin ("It's okay to go ahead and sin; you know God will forgive you") or to become fatalistic and hopeless over sin ("You've blown it, and God will never forgive you; you might as well go ahead and keep on sinning").

John wanted believers to know that if they sinned, they were to run to God not from Him, and that they did not need to fear His wrath or condemnation. He wrote, "Don't sin, but if you do...". The good news it is that God doesn't hate us, reject us, or abandon us when we sin. He continues to love us and beckon us unto Himself. Remember, repentance is not only turning from sin; repentance is turning to God and the hope and new possibilities He has for us. That is grace! So how does a believer walk in God's wonderful plan?

So we are lying if we say we have fellowship with God but go on living in spiritual darkness; we are not practicing the truth. But if we are living in the light, as God is in the light, then we have fellowship with each other, and the blood of Jesus, his Son, cleanses us from all sin.

If we claim we have no sin, we are only fooling ourselves and not living in the truth. But if we confess our sins to him, he is faithful and just to forgive us our sins and to cleanse us from all wickedness.

1 John 1:6-9 NLT

John is talking about fellowship with God versus fellowship with darkness, a familiar theme from his fellow apostles:

You cannot drink the cup of the Lord and the cup of demons; you cannot partake of the Lord's table and of the table of demons.

1 Corinthians 10:21

Do you not know that friendship with the world is enmity with God? Whoever therefore wants to be a friend of the world makes himself an enemy of God.

James 4:4

If we live in the light, we have fellowship with "each other." Who is the "each other" John is referring to? Is he talking about a group of believers fellowshipping with one another? While it is true that if we are all walking in the light we will have fellowship with each other, it appears in context that he is talking about the believer and God fellowshipping with "each other."

When we walk in the light, not only do we experience and enjoy fellowship with God, but we are told that "the blood of Jesus, his Son, cleanses us from all sin." The Amplified version says the cleansing experienced by the believer is present and continuous: "And the blood of Jesus Christ His Son cleanses (removes) us from all sin and guilt [keeps us cleansed...]." What an amazing and liberating truth!

This answers so many questions, such as, "What if I committed a sin but didn't know it was a sin?" or "What if I forgot to confess a particular sin?" As long as we're walking in the light (and we can only assume this means we are walking in the light we have), then there is a continual cleansing taking place, even if we are unaware we have sinned in a certain area.

In verse 8, John tells us we should not deceive ourselves into believing our lives are flawlessly perfect, sinless to a point where we no longer need forgiveness. Then he proceeds to say,

> *If we [freely] admit that we have sinned and confess our sins, He is faithful and just (true to His own nature and promises) and will forgive our sins [dismiss our lawlessness] and [continuously] cleanse us from all unrighteousness [everything not in conformity to His will in purpose, thought, and action].*

> 1 John 1:9 AMP

How joyful and liberating all of this is—and an amazing source of security! God has given us His light, His power, and His ability to keep us from sinning, but He understands that we are still human and may miss the mark of perfection from time to time. If we are unaware of a particular sin, we don't have to worry about that because the blood of Jesus is continuously cleansing us from all sin. If we sin and know it, He wants us to be honest with Him, truthfully acknowledge our fault, and receive the cleansing He so freely offers! This is not living in sin-consciousness; it is living with a tender, conscientious heart, always ready to receive our Father's abundant grace whenever we need it.

The idea has been presented that the first chapter of 1 John (including verse 9) wasn't really addressed to Christians; instead, it is purported that 1 John 1 was written to unbelievers or to Gnostics. There is nothing in the text to substantiate this thought. Several New Testament epistles address various errors in the body of Christ, but all are written to believers, and 1 John 1 is no exception. The Corinthians lived in a very lascivious and hedonistic society, the Galatians had been influenced by legalism, and some in Colosse had been affected by asceticism, but Paul wrote each epistle to the believers in those cities.

Likewise, 1 John was written in a time when Gnosticism influenced the thinking and beliefs of some, but the entire epistle—from the first verse to the closing verse of the book—was written to Christians. John was not a Gnostic, so he assuredly was not grouping himself with them. He was not saying:

- "So we [Gnostics] are lying if we say we have fellowship with God but go on living in spiritual darkness" (1 John 1:6, my paraphrase).

- "If we [Gnostics] are living in the light, as God is in the light, then we have fellowship with each other" (1 John 1:7, my paraphrase).

- "If we [Gnostics] confess our sins to him, he is faithful and just to forgive us our sins and to cleanse us from all wickedness" (1 John 1:9, my paraphrase).

It does not make biblical sense to say that if a Gnostic (or any un-saved person) confesses his sins that he will be saved either. The confession that saves the sinner is the confession of Jesus Christ as Lord (see Romans 10:9-10).

The Bible Knowledge Commentary states:

> In modern times some have occasionally denied that a Christian needs to confess his sins and ask forgiveness. It is claimed that a believer already has forgiveness in Christ (Ephesians 1:7). But this point of view confuses the perfect position which a Christian has in God's Son (by which he is even "seated . . . with Him in the heavenly realms" [Ephesians 2:6]) with his needs as a failing individual on Earth. What is considered in 1 John 1:9 may be described as "familial" forgiveness. It is perfectly understandable how a son may need to ask his father to forgive him for his faults while at the same time his position within the family is not in jeopardy. A Christian who never asks his heavenly Father for forgiveness for his sins can hardly have much sensitivity to the ways in which he grieves his Father. First John 1:9 is not spoken to the unsaved, and the effort to turn it into a soteriological affirmation is misguided.[5]

Let's Get Practical

Sin is a serious issue, but once we have confessed sin and repented, God does not want us wallowing in the guilt of past sins. He has provided cleansing and forgiveness for us, and he wants us to gratefully receive that and resume walking in the light!

If you are not aware of any sin in your life, then keep walking in the light and know that even if you have inadvertently sinned and are una-ware of it, He will be cleansing you all along, and you can always thank

Him for this. If you are aware of having committed a sin you have not acknowledged to Him, go ahead and do that right now. Be honest with Him and thank Him because He is faithful and just to forgive your sins and to cleanse you from all unrighteousness. Align yourself with His will and His purpose, and know that He has something far better for you than sin could ever offer.

God's grace in the death of Jesus on the Cross makes repentance possible, not unnecessary. Confession brings liberty, releasing overcoming power. And forgiveness and cleansing are received with joy.

All of this is available because our God is gracious. When we need to repent of something, our confession and repentance should be grace-based and faith-based, not shame-based or fear-based. This means we come to God knowing He has continued to love us in spite of our sin, and that He cleanses us. He is not moved by our groveling and belittling ourselves, but by the blood of His Son Jesus.

Grace doesn't take the place of confession of sin, but it certainly influences how we confess our sin. Because of grace, we don't wallow in our sin, we don't let guilt linger and dominate us, and we don't allow shame and condemnation to rule over us.

We do not confess our sins to inform God. Just as Jesus knew Peter would deny Him ahead of time, God knew that we would sin and would need forgiveness before we were ever born. Nevertheless, He loves us and called us to be His children anyway. David said it best in the psalms:

> *You see me when I travel*
> *and when I rest at home.*
> *You know everything I do.*
> *You know what I am going to say*
> *even before I say it, LORD.*

Psalm 139:3-4 NLT

You saw me before I was born.

Every day of my life was recorded in your book.

Every moment was laid out

before a single day had passed.

How precious are your thoughts about me, O God.

They cannot be numbered!

Psalm 139:16-17 NLT

Another way of saying this is that we don't acknowledge our sins because God needs information; we acknowledge our sins because we need to receive the release of forgiveness and freedom from guilt, condemnation, and shame His grace provided for us on the Cross.

We do not confess our sins so God will love us again. God never stops loving us, even when we sin. Our sin doesn't change God, but it creates problems for us. Nevertheless, God's love is not fickle, based on our perfection or lack thereof; His love is steady and stable because it is based on who He is, and He is unchanging. He is love.

We do not confess our sins to earn forgiveness. Earning is not the issue; receiving is. Jesus earned or procured our forgiveness on the Cross. When we acknowledge our sin, we are simply responding in faith to God's Word to receive the glorious, wonderful, free gift of cleansing and forgiveness He extends.

How many have "fallen on their own sword" when they should have fallen into His grace? So don't let past sins become your downfall. God's grace is greater than anything you have done or might do in the future. Because of His grace, you can walk in continual cleansing from all sin, confident yet humbled by His amazing gift.

Questions for Reflection and Discussion:

- What was new and fresh to you?

- What reinforced the understanding you already had?

- What challenged your previous or current understanding?

- Do you believe you are fairly well balanced in your understanding of God's truths in your life? Are there any issues in the Bible that you over-emphasize or under-emphasize?

- Review the list in Chapter 19 under the subhead: **Grace and…** and note how God's grace is influencing you in many of these other areas. Where do you sense His influence the most? The least?

- How do you define confession and repentance?

- What does it mean to bring forth fruit worthy of repentance?

- How does repentance affect your relationship with the Lord?

- Is it possible for a believer to repent without confession? Why or why not?

- Why does God correct His children when they err?

- If God's grace makes repentance possible, what does that mean to you?

Part Seven

One More Thing You Should Know...

Chapter 24

GRACE AND GLORY

God of grace and God of glory,
On Thy people pour Thy power.
Crown Thine ancient church's story,
Bring her bud to glorious flower.

—Harry E. Fosdick

Here are some of the specific scriptures where grace and glory are connected:

> *The LORD will give grace and glory...*
>
> Psalm 84:11

> *...an ornament of grace; A crown of glory...*
>
> Proverbs 4:9

> *...to the praise of the glory of His grace.*
>
> Ephesians 1:6

> *And the Word became flesh and dwelt among us, and we beheld His glory, the glory as of the only begotten of the Father, full of grace and truth.*
>
> John 1:14

We have access by faith into this grace in which we stand, and rejoice in hope of the glory of God.

Romans 5:2

...that grace, having spread through the many, may cause thanksgiving to abound to the glory of God.

2 Corinthians 4:15

But may the God of all grace, who called us to His eternal glory by Christ Jesus....

1 Peter 5:10

When we see grace and glory used together many times, we should investigate the nature of their connection. Is it just a coincidence? Did the writers of the Bible just need some flowery, spiritual-sounding words to go together? I believe there is a definite and purposeful connection between the two.

The Hebrew word frequently translated glory (*kabowd*) refers to God's honor, splendor, dignity, and abundance.[1] It is from a root word (*kabad*) that means heavy or weighty.[2] This sheds insight as to why Paul, writing in the New Testament, referred to "a far more exceeding and eternal weight of glory" in 2 Corinthians 4:17.

In Exodus 33:18, Moses said to God, "Please show me Your glory." What an amazing request! He was asking God, "Please show me Your glory, Your honor, Your splendor, Your dignity, Your abundance." There was obviously a weightiness or heaviness to God's glory that was too much for Moses any other human to handle, because God replies,

*"I will make all My **goodness** pass before you, and I will proclaim the name of the Lord before you. I will be **gracious** to whom I will be gracious, and I will have **compassion** on whom I will have compassion." But He said, "You cannot see My face; for no man shall see Me, and*

live." And the LORD said, "Here is a place by Me, and you shall stand
on the rock. So it shall be, while My glory passes by, that I will put you
in the cleft of the rock, and will cover you with My hand while I pass
by. Then I will take away My hand, and you shall see My back; but My
face shall not be seen.

Exodus 33:19-23

In these verses, God identifies His glory with His goodness, grace, and compassion. It is consistent with His nature that all of these are associated with one another. There also seems to be an element of "degrees" involved. Moses could see the backside of God, but were he to see His face, the Lord said he would not have been able to live.

The word for glory in the Greek language is *doxa*, which is where we get the word "doxology." Glory refers to dignity, splendor, honor, brightness, majesty, and praise.

God's glory is seen in strong manifestation in Luke's account of the transfiguration:

He [Jesus] took Peter, John, and James and went up on the mountain
to pray. **As He prayed, the appearance of His face was altered, and**
His robe became white and glistening. *And behold, two men talked*
with Him, who were Moses and Elijah, who appeared in **glory** *and*
spoke of His decease which He was about to accomplish at Jerusalem.
But Peter and those with him were heavy with sleep; and when they
were fully awake, **they saw His glory** *and the two men who stood*
with Him.

Luke 9:28-32 (bold mine)

Like the Old Testament, the idea of varying degrees of glory is clearly explained by Paul in 1 Corinthians 15, the chapter in which he expounded upon the resurrection of the dead. Right before he said our physical bodies will be "raised in glory" at the resurrection, he said,

There are heavenly bodies (sun, moon, and stars) and there are earth-ly bodies (men, animals, and plants), but the beauty and glory of the heavenly bodies is of one kind, while the beauty and glory of earthly bodies is a different kind.

The sun is glorious in one way, the moon is glorious in another way, and the stars are glorious in their own [distinctive] way; for one star differs from and surpasses another in its beauty and brilliance.

1 Corinthians 15:40-41 AMP

As we move into 2 Corinthians, Paul contrasts the Old Covenant with the New Covenant, and he points out that the glory of the New Covenant is much greater than the glory of the Old Covenant. Again, the idea of degrees of glory is conveyed.

*The old way, with laws etched in stone, led to death, though it began with such **glory** that the people of Israel could not bear to look at Moses' face. For his face shone with the **glory** of God, even though the brightness was already fading away. Shouldn't we expect far greater **glory** under the new way, now that the Holy Spirit is giving life? If the old way, which brings condemnation, was **glorious**, how much more **glorious** is the new way, which makes us right with God! In fact, **that first glory was not glorious at all compared with the overwhelming glory of the new way.** So if the old way, which has been replaced, was **glorious**, how much more **glorious** is the new, which remains forever!*

2 Corinthians 3:7-11 NLT (bold mine)

So the New Covenant, which is based upon the grace of God, is a covenant of "overwhelming glory." When we are born again, the grace of God literally gives us the ability to behold and partake of the glory of God. Yet some Christians are almost afraid of the glory because their primary association with the word is from the Old Testament:

I am the LORD, that is My name;

And My glory I will not give to another,

Nor My praise to carved images.

Isaiah 42:8

It is understandable and appropriate that we would never want to take God's glory unto ourselves in a vainglorious or idolatrous way. Nevertheless, we must harmonize this verse in Isaiah with the other scriptures in which God said He has already given us His glory. For example:

"I do not pray for these alone, but also for those who will believe in Me through their word.

"And **the glory which You gave Me I have given them,** *that they may be one just as We are one."*

John 17:20,22 (bold mine)

Did God (speaking through Isaiah) and Jesus (as recorded in the book of John) contradict each other? God said He would not give His glory to another, and Jesus said He had given His glory to us. There is no contradiction. Who was the "another" to whom God referred in Isaiah? If you look at it in context, He was speaking of false gods and idols. If I were to say, "This is my checkbook, and I will not give it to another," I would mean strangers and those I had no reason to trust. However, I would not be including my wife! She can have my checkbook anytime she wants it, because we are one; she is not "another." So God in Isaiah 42:8 is not talking about His children.

Actually, God had already given His glory to His own children when He created them. Consider this:

When I look at the night sky and see the work of your fingers—

the moon and the stars you set in place—

> *what are mere mortals that you should think about them,*
> *human beings that you should care for them?*
> **Yet you made them only a little lower than God**
> **and crowned them with glory and honor.**
> *You gave them charge of everything you made,*
> *putting all things under their authority.*
>
> Psalm 8:3-6 NLT (bold mine)

Isn't that amazing! When God created Adam and Eve, He didn't create them as "worms of the dust." He made them just a little lower than Himself and He crowned them with glory and honor! Of course, mankind lost much in the fall, but Jesus came to deliver us from sin and to restore us to God. When we were reunited with God, we were once again partakers of His glory, His good opinion of us was restored in Christ.

Not only do we see the connection between grace and glory in the Scriptures, but many individuals throughout history have noticed the link as well.

> Grace is but glory begun, and glory is but grace perfected.
>
> —Jonathan Edwards[3]

> Grace is young glory.
>
> —Alexander Peden[4]

> Grace...is glory in its infancy.
>
> —S. Rutherford[5]

> Perhaps in reality the grace and the glory are one. Perhaps God's grace is like a wondrous tree, of which His glory is the fruit.
>
> —Ray Charles Jarman[6]

God Has Ordained His People to be Glorious

For God knew his people in advance, and he chose them to become like his Son, so that his Son would be the firstborn among many brothers and sisters. And having chosen them, he called them to come to him. And having called them, he gave them right standing with himself. And having given them right standing, **he gave them his glory.**

Romans 8:29-30 NLT (bold mine)

Christ loved the church. He gave up his life for her to make her holy and clean, washed by the cleansing of God's word. **He did this to present her to himself as a glorious church** *without a spot or wrinkle or any other blemish. Instead, she will be holy and without fault.*

Ephesians 5:25-27 NLT (bold mine)

...that the name of our Lord Jesus Christ may be **glorified** *in you, and you in Him, according to the grace of our God and the Lord Jesus Christ.*

2 Thessalonians 1:12 (bold mine)

Whenever someone turns to the Lord, the veil is taken away.

So all of us who have had that veil removed can see and reflect the glory of the Lord. And the Lord—who is the Spirit—makes us more and more like him as we are changed into his glorious image.

2 Corinthians 3:16,18 NLT

If you are reproached for the name of Christ, blessed are you, for **the Spirit of glory and of God rests upon you.** *On their part He is blasphemed, but on your part He is glorified.*

1 Peter 4:14 (bold mine)

His divine power has granted to us all things that pertain to life and godliness, through the knowledge of him who **called us by glory and virtue.**

2 Peter 1:3 ESV (bold mine)

Even our physical bodies will ultimately be touched by His glory:

He will take our weak mortal bodies and change them into glorious bodies like his own, using the same power with which he will bring everything under his control.

Philippians 3:21 NLT

Paul also talks about the saints receiving their glorious physical bodies in 1 Corinthians 15:50-57.

Perhaps you have already been aware of these truths—that God has not only flooded our lives with His wonderful grace, but He has given us His glory and made us partakers of His divine nature. We are His children, and God wants His children to be glorious like Himself. When we receive this truth properly, walking in the light of all the Scripture, we will never become proud, haughty, or arrogant about this. God does not share His glory with us so that we can become "little gods" independent of Him; rather, He invests His grace and glory into our lives so He can receive glory from us!

From the beginning of time until now, God has been pouring out blessings and sowing His grace into humanity. In the book of Revelation, we see God reaping the harvest of which He is worthy and deserving. In Revelation 4:10-11, we have a picture of the elders in Heaven, and no one is strutting around or impressed with themselves or their accomplishments. They are casting their crowns before the throne of God, saying,

> *"You are worthy, O Lord our God,*
> *   to receive glory and honor and power.*
> *For you created all things,*
> *   and they exist because you created what you pleased."*

Revelation 4:11 NLT

In the next chapter of Revelation, John sees a scroll in the right hand of the One who sat upon the throne. He weeps, "because no one was found worthy to open and read the scroll, or to look at it" (Revelation 5:4). What happens next reveals much about God's eternal plan.

> *One of the elders said to me, "Do not weep. Behold, the Lion of the tribe of Judah, the Root of David, has prevailed to open the scroll and to loose its seven seals."*
>
> Revelation 5:5

The elders then worship Jesus the Lamb because of His worthiness and His accomplishments; they glorify the One who had made them to be kings and priests unto God.

> *And they sang a new song, saying:*
> *"You are worthy to take the scroll,*
> *And to open its seals;*
> *For You were slain,*
> *And have redeemed us to God by Your blood*
> *Out of every tribe and tongue and people and nation,*
> *And have made us kings and priests to our God;*
> *And we shall reign on the earth."*
>
> Revelation 5:9-10

Even though the elders and all the other saints in Heaven were glorified, they completely understood their rank and assignment relative to God and the Lord Jesus. They understood God's glory was inherent and intrinsic, while their righteousness and glory had been imparted to them as gifts from the graciousness and goodness of God. The glory they had received in no way competed with or diminished God's glory because they returned it to Him through worship and praise. This is God's desire and purpose for our lives.

*For everything comes from him and exists by his power and is intended
for his glory. All glory to him forever.*

Romans 11:36 NLT

What Does This Mean to Your Life Today?

Grace and glory are intimately connected because God's grace produces glory in your life. You now "reflect the glory of the Lord," and He makes you "more and more like him as [you] are changed into his glorious image" (2 Corinthians 3:18 NLT). I believe knowing this has profound significance in your life.

Understanding God's grace and glory radically challenges any religious, traditional thinking that may have influenced you in the past. You may have been raised thinking you were "just an old, unworthy sinner" or a "worm of the dust." That doesn't speak very highly of God's grace if that is all it produces in you. No, His grace produces His glory in you! You and I are to live lives that reflect God's dignity, splendor, honor, brightness, majesty, and praise.

Further, it is through God's grace and glory that He provides you the power and incentive to live in a way that reflects your royal inheritance and glorious identity. We referred earlier to 2 Peter 1:3, which says God has called you to, "his own glory and virtue." The next verse says, "He has given us his very great and precious promises, so that through them you may participate in the divine nature, having escaped the corruption in the world caused by desires" (2 Peter 1:4 NIV[11]).

Questions for Reflection and Discussion:

- What was new and fresh to you?

- What reinforced the understanding you already had?

- What challenged your previous or current understanding?

- How did the teaching in this chapter affect your understanding of God's glory in your life?

- What is it about the grace and glory of God that causes us to know that we are not "just an old, unworthy sinner" or a "worm of the dust"?

- What are some of the reasons God has allowed us to be partakers of His glory? How do you view the operation of His glory in your life?

A FINAL WORD

We have seen the pre-eminence of the doctrine of grace in the Word of God, so we know it is vitally important that we understand it. Thus, we studied what God's grace is and what it is not. We looked at grace in terms of its far-reaching influence and its manifold expressions. We have learned:

- Grace is not about what we achieve, but what we receive.

- Grace has nothing to do with us earning salvation, but it has everything to do with our expressing the salvation God gave us freely through Jesus Christ.

- Grace is not something we cease to experience after being born again, but it is available to us for the duration of our Christian walk. Grace empowers and inspires how we live for Him.

Grace means so much to so many different people:

- To those who are without God and without hope, grace is the unconditional love of God offering the gift of forgiveness and eternal life.

- To every prodigal in the pigpen—the ones who walked away from the Father's good plan—grace is the opportunity for complete restoration and another chance.

- To believers struggling with habits, bondages, and sins of the flesh, grace is not only a release from guilt, condemnation, and shame, but it is empowerment to rise above the power of sin and walk worthy of the calling of God.

- To Christians overwhelmed with the pressures and problems of life, grace is the continuous infusion of power, strength, and might; it is God's sufficiency to bring them victoriously through life's challenges.

- To believers struggling financially, grace is the revelation that God is Jehovah Jireh—the Lord our Provider. Grace reveals God's love for us: spiritually, mentally, emotionally, physically, socially, and financially. By His grace, all our needs can be met and we can be generous toward others.

- To individuals wondering if they can be fruitful and productive in their Christian lives, grace imparts spiritual gifts and abilities, equipping them with tools for effective service.

We have discussed not only what grace provides, but also what grace produces. Grace provides for us what we could have never obtained apart from God's benevolence and generosity. Grace produces in and through us what we could have never generated by our own fleshly efforts.

- God's grace releases us from the burdens we were never created to bear and empowers us to carry out the responsibilities we were created to fulfill.

- God's grace is never an excuse to disobey God or cease being a committed disciple of the Lord Jesus Christ; rather, it is empowerment to become everything God has ordained us to become and to do the things He has called us to do.

- God's grace is not a cop-out from Christian disciplines; rather, it is a catalyst enabling us to fulfill all God has planned and desires in our lives.

- Grace is not a spiritual hammock in which we lazily abandon and abdicate spiritual responsibilities; rather, God's grace is a launching pad that propels us into a life of obedience, consecration, and Christlikeness.

As we partake of grace, more grace, manifold grace, and multiplied grace, our lives will not be lived independently from God, but our lives will reflect the spiritual union that God has paid so high a price to establish with us. May we cease striving in the flesh, and may we experience and enjoy the grace-based life He has ordained for us, a life that is guided by His Word and empowered by His Spirit. May we find our lives so completely immersed and entwined in Him that we say with the apostle Paul, "By the grace of God I am what I am" (1 Corinthians 15:10).

ENDNOTES

Chapter 1 God's DNA in You

1 Dr. Paul Brand and Philip Yancey, *Fearfully and Wonderfully Made.* (Grand Rapids, MI. Zondervan, 1981), Page 45.

2 J.F. Walvoord, R.B. Zuck & Dallas Theological Seminary, (1983-c1985), *The Bible knowledge commentary : An exposition of the scriptures.* (Wheaton, IL: Victor Books), Volume 1, Page 29.

Chapter 3 Grace in Hello and Goodbye

[1]James Strong, *Exhaustive Concordance of the Bible, "Hebrew and Chaldee Dictionary"* (Nashville, TN: Thomas Nelson Publishers, 1984), #7965.

Chapter 4 The Benevolent Judge

[1] J. Clyde Turner, *The Gospel of the Grace of God* (Nashville, TN: Broadman Press, 1943), p. 16.

[2]Spiros Zodhiates, *Hebrew-Greek Key Word Study Bible "Lexical Aids to the Old Testament"* (Chattanooga, TN: AMG Publishers, 1984, 1991), #2580, #2603.

[3]W. H. Griffith Thomas, *Grace and Power* (New York, NY: Fleming H. Revell Company, 1916), p. 22.

[4]Spiros Zodhiates, *The Complete Word Study Dictionary: New Testament* (Chattanooga, TN: AMG Publishers, 1992), #5485.

[5]James Moffatt, *Grace in the New Testament* (London, England: Hodder and Stoughton, 1931) p. 25.

[6]Mark Water, *The New Encyclopedia of Christian Quotations* (Grand Rapids, MI: Baker Books, 2000), p. 446.

[7]http://christian-quotes.ochristian.com/Alexander-Whyte-Quotes/

[8]Mark Water, *The New Encyclopedia of Christian Quotations*, p. 444.

[9]Richard Allen Farmer, *How Sweet the Sound* (Downer's Grove, IL: Intervarsity Press, 2003), p. 83.

[10]http://thegracetabernacle.org/quotes/Grace-Defined.htm

[11]W. H. Griffith Thomas, *Grace and Power*, p. 89.

Chapter 5 Five Expressions of God's Grace

[1]Thomas A Kempis, *The Imitation of Christ* (www.forgottenbooks.com: Forgotten Books, 1886, 2007), p. 58.

Chapter 6 What Grace Is Not

[1]http://www.gracecorning.org/quotes-about-grace

[2]http://www.michelangelo-gallery.com/quotes.aspx

[3]http://www.scrollpublishing.com/store/Bonhoeffer.html

[4]Ibid.

Chapter 7 The Manifold Grace of God

[1]W. H. Griffith Thomas, *Grace and Power,* p. 86-88.

[2]The Online Etymology Dictionary (http://www.etymonline.com/index.
php?term=manifold)

Chapter 8 The Basics

[1]http://thegracetabernacle.org/quotes/Salvation-Grace_Alone.htm

[2]L. E. Barton, *Amazing Grace* (Boston, MA: The Christopher Publishing House, 1954).

[3]F. F. Bruce, from a lecture delivered in the John Rylands University Library of Manchester on Wednesday, the 15th of November, 1972. http://www.biblicalstudies.org.uk/pdf/bjrl/problems-5_bruce.pdf

Chapter 9 Saved From What?

[1]Sinclair B. Ferguson, *Grow in Grace* (Carlisle, PA: The Banner of Truth Trust, 1989), p. 57.

[2]C.S. Lewis, *The Problem of Pain* (New York, NY: Harper Collins, 1940), pp. 119-20.

[3]William E. Evans, *The Great Doctrines of the Bible* (Chicago: The Bible Institute Colportage Association, 1912) p. 79.

[4]http://christian-quotes.ochristian.com/D.L.-Moody-Quotes/page-11.shtml

[5]Mark Water, *The New Encyclopedia of Christian Quotations*, p. 241.

[6]H. A. Ironside, *Expository Notes on the Gospel of Matthew* (Neptune, NJ: Loizeaux Brothers, 1994), p. 384.

[7]H. A. Ironside, *Charge That to My Account* (Chicago, IL: Moody Press, 1931), p. 66.

[8]http://biblestudy.churches.net/CCEL/S/SPURGEON/TILL_HE_/GIVEREST.HTM

Chapter 10 But I'm a Law-Abiding Citizen!

[1]http://www.jesus-is-savior.com/Great%20Men%20of%20God/dwight_moody-quotes.html

Chapter 11 From Shadow to Substance

[1]Mark Water, *The New Encyclopedia of Christian Quotations*, p. 444.

Chapter 13 Sanctifying Grace

[1]Mark Water, *The New Encyclopedia of Christian Quotations*, p. 478.

[2]http://www.studylight.org/isb/bible.cgi?query=tit+2%3A12&section=0&it=kjv&oq=tit
%25202%3A11&ot=bhs&nt=na&new=1&nb=tit&ng=2&ncc=2

[3]Mark Water, *The New Encyclopedia of Christian Quotations*, p. 365.

Chapter 14 Strengthening Grace

[1]http://thinkexist.com/quotation/fatigue_makes_cowards_of_us_all/149882.html

[2]Dennis Hester, *The Vance Havner Quote Book* (Grand Rapids, MI: Baker Book House, 1986), p. 68.

Chapter 15 Sharing Grace

[1]http://christianpf.com/quotes-on-giving/

[2]http://www.globalissues.org/article/26/poverty-facts-and-stats

[3]W. H. Griffith Thomas, *Grace and Power* (New York, NY: Fleming H. Revell Company, 1916), p. 84.

[4]http://www.goodreads.com/quotes/show/151380

[5]http://www.ctlibrary.com/le/1996/fall/6l4068.html

[6]William Barclay, *Daily Study Bible Series: The Gospel of John - Volume 2, Revised Edition* (Louisville, KY: Westminster John Knox Press, 1976), p. 262.

[7]Gerald L. Borchert, *The New American Commentary: John 12-21* (Nashville, TN: Broadman Press, 2002), p. 280.

[8]Spiros Zodhiates, *The Complete Word Study Dictionary: New Testament*, #2431.

[9]http://www.moravian.org/believe/covenant_christian_living.pdf (Section II, Point 10)

[10]http://www.wholesomewords.org/missions/msquotes.html

[11]Spiros Zodhiates, *The Complete Word Study Dictionary: New Testament*, #1183.

[12]http://www.christianitytoday.com/ct/2008/december/10.24.html

Chapter 16 Serving Grace

[1]G. L. Bray, *Ancient Christian Commentary on Scripture, New Testament VII, 1-2 Corinthians* (Downers Grove, IL: InterVarsity Press, 1999), p. 153.

[2]Cleon L. Rogers Jr. and Cleon L. Rogers III, *The New Linguistic and Exegetical Key to the Greek New Testament* (Grand Rapids, MI: Zondervan Publishing House, 1998) p. 385.

[3]Mark Water, *The New Encyclopedia of Christian Quotations*, p. 230.

[4]Spiros Zodhiates, *The Complete Word Study Dictionary: New Testament*, #4164.

[5]Frederick William Danker, *A Greek-English Lexicon Of The New Testament And Other Early Christian Literature, Third Edition* (Chicago, IL: University of Chicago Press, 2000), p. 1080.

[6]Warren W. Wiersbe, *The Bible Expository Commentary* (Wheaton, IL: Victor Books, Electronic Edition, 1996), Comment on Romans 12:3-6.

[7]http://www.christianitytoday.com/ch/131christians/evangelistsandapologists/moody.html

[8]Glen Clark, *The Man Who Talks with Flowers* (Saint Paul, MN: Macalester Park Publishing Company, 1939), p. 37.

Chapter 17 The Joy of More Grace

[1]Sinclair B. Ferguson, *By Grace Alone: How the Grace of God Amazes Me* (Lake Mary, FL: Reformation Trust Publishing, 2010), p. xv.

[2]Sinclair B. Ferguson, *Feed My Sheep: A Passionate Plea for Preaching* (Lake Mary, FL: Reformation Trust Publishing, 2008), p. 113.

[3]D. A. Carson, R. T. France, J. A. Motyer, G. J. Wenham, editors, *The New Bible Commentary: 21st Century Edition* (Downers Grove, IL: Intervarsity Press, Fourth Edition 1994), Comment on John 1:16.

[4]Archibald Thomas Robertson, *Word Pictures in the New Testament* (Nashville, TN: Broadman Press, 1932), Comment on John 1:16

[5]Mark J. Edwards, *Ancient Christian Commentary on Scripture: New Testament VIII: Galatians, Ephesians, and Philippians* (Downers Grove, IL: Intervarsity Press, 2005). P. 133.

[7]James Strong, *Exhaustive Concordance of the Bible*, "Greek Dictionary of the New Testament" (Nashville, TN: Thomas Nelson Publishers, 1984), #498.

[8]http://www.jesus-is-savior.com/Great%20Men%20of%20God/dwight_moody-quotes.htm

[9]http://www.christianitytoday.com/ct/2006/julyweb-only/130-52.0.html

Chapter 19 Complementary Attributes

[1]http://www.quotedb.com/quotes/2518

[2]This traditional spiritual song was based on Ezekiel 37:17-14.

Chapter 20 Recognizing Our Filters

[1]http://www.giga-usa.com/quotes/authors/ambrose_1_a001.htm

Chapter 21 Repentance and Confession

[1]Ralph Earle, *Word Meanings in the New Testament* (Peabody, MA: Hendrickson Publishers, 1974), p. 30.

[2]Joseph H. Thayer, *Thayer's Greek-English Lexicon of the New Testament* (Grand Rapids, MI: Baker Book House, 1977), pp. 405-406.

[3]Rick Renner, *A Light in Darkness: Seven Messages to the Seven Churches* (Tulsa, OK: Teach All Nations, 2010), pp. 320-321.

[4]William Douglas Chamberlain, *The Meaning of Repentance* (Philadelphia, PA: The Westminster Press, 1943) p. 22.

[5]Ibid., p. 43.

[6]Ibid., p. 47.

[7]Spiros Zodhiates, *The Complete Word Study Dictionary: New Testament*, #3670.

[8]Warren W. Wiersbe, *The Bible Expository Commentary*, Comment on 1 John 1:9.

Chapter 23 What Did the Apostles Say?

[1]Helen H. Lemmel, "Turn Your Eyes Upon Jesus," 1922.

[2]William Douglas Chamberlain, *The Meaning of Repentance*, p. 52.

[3]http://www.allthingswilliam.com/forgiveness.html

[4]Spiros Zodhiates, *The Complete Word Study Dictionary: New Testament*, #2434.

[5]J. F. Walvoord and R. B. Zuck, editors, *The Bible Knowledge Commentary: An Exposition of the Scriptures* (Wheaton, IL: Victor Books, 1983, 1985), Vol. 2, Page 886.

Chapter 24 Grace and Glory

[1]http://www.blueletterbible.org/lang/lexicon/lexicon.cfm?Strongs=H3519&t=KJV

[2]http://www.blueletterbible.org/lang/lexicon/lexicon.cfm?Strongs=H3513&t=KJV

[3]http://christian-quotes.ochristian.com/christian-quotes_ochristian.cgi?find=Christian-quotes-by-Jonathan+Edwards-on-Grace

[4]Mark Water, *The New Encyclopedia of Christian Quotations*, p. 230.

[5]Ibid.

[6]Ray Charles Jarman and Carmen Bensen, The Grace and the Glory of God (Plainfield, New Jersey: Logos International, 1968), p 7.

About the Author

Bible teacher and author Tony Cooke has been serving the Body of Christ in various capacities since 1980. His passion for teaching the Bible has taken him to more than forty-five states and twenty-two nations.

His website (www.tonycooke.org) reaches pastors, missionaries, and other church leaders in 175 nations with encouraging and helpful ministerial resources.

Tony was involved in pastoral ministry for more than twenty years, and served as an instructor and the dean of Rhema Bible Training Center. He also served for thirteen years as the director of an International Ministerial Association.

Since 2002, Tony and his wife Lisa have traveled full-time with an assignment of "strengthening churches and leaders."

In addition to being a 1981 graduate of Rhema Bible Training Center, Tony studied Religion at Butler University and received a Bachelor of Science degree in Church Ministries from North Central University.

Tony and his wife, Lisa, reside in Broken Arrow, Oklahoma, and are the parents of two adult children, Laura and Andrew.

> To receive free monthly teaching from Tony Cooke, visit www.tonycooke.org and sign up to receive Tony's e-newsletter.

The Prayer of Salvation

God loves you—no matter who you are, no matter what your past. God loves you so much that He gave His one and only begotten Son for you. The Bible tells us that "...whoever believes in him shall not perish but have eternal life" (John 3:16 NIV). Jesus laid down His life and rose again so that we could spend eternity with Him in heaven and experience His absolute best on Earth. If you would like to make Jesus the Lord of your life, say the following prayer out loud and mean it from your heart.

> *Dear Heavenly Father,*
>
> *I come to You in the Name of Jesus.*
>
> *Your Word says, "...the one who comes to Me I will by no means cast out" (John 6:37), so I know You won't cast me out, but You take me in and I thank You for it.*
>
> *You said in Your Word, "Whoever shall call upon the name of the Lord shall be saved" (Romans 10:13). I am calling on Your Name, so I know You have saved me now.*
>
> *You also said "...if you confess with your mouth the Lord Jesus, and believe in your heart that God has raised him from the dead, you will be saved. For with the heart one believes unto righteousness; and with the mouth confession is made unto salvation" (Romans 10:9-10). I believe in my heart Jesus Christ is the Son of God. I believe that He was raised from the dead for my justification, and I confess Him now as my Lord.*
>
> *Because Your Word says, "...with the heart one believes unto righteousness..." and I do believe with my heart, I have now become the righteousness of God in Christ (2 Corinthians 5:21)...And I am saved!*

If you prayed the prayer to receive Jesus Christ as your Lord and Savior, please contact us on the web at www.harrisonhouse.com to receive a free book. Or you may write to us at:

Harrison House • P.O. Box 35035 • Tulsa, Oklahoma 74153

The Harrison House Vision

Proclaiming the truth and the power of the gospel of Jesus Christ with excellence;
Challenging Christians to live victoriously, grow spiritually, and know God intimately.

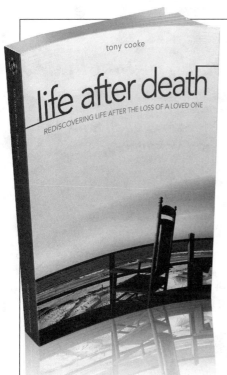

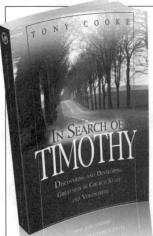